THIS, THAT,
AND
THE
OTHER THING

THIS, THAT, AND THE OTHER THING

RICHARD ALTHAGE

XULON ELITE

Xulon Press Elite
555 Winderley Pl, Suite 225
Maitland, FL 32751
407.339.4217
www.xulonpress.com

© 2023 by Richard Althage

All rights reserved solely by the author. The author guarantees all contents are original and do not infringe upon the legal rights of any other person or work. No part of this book may be reproduced in any form without the permission of the author.

Due to the changing nature of the Internet, if there are any web addresses, links, or URLs included in this manuscript, these may have been altered and may no longer be accessible. The views and opinions shared in this book belong solely to the author and do not necessarily reflect those of the publisher. The publisher therefore disclaims responsibility for the views or opinions expressed within the work.

Unless otherwise indicated, Scripture quotations taken from the Holy Bible, New International Version (NIV). Copyright © 1973, 1978, 1984, 2011 by Biblica, Inc.™. Used by permission. All rights reserved.

Paperback ISBN-13: 978-1-66288-583-9
Ebook ISBN-13: 978-1-66288-584-6

Note to My Readers

I'm an early riser, likely because I'm thinking all night. Frequently, those thoughts are about books: books I've written, books I'm reading, and books that I'll want to write. It's not unusual for me to get up at any hour to write a note, lest I forget my subconscious ideas. So, *This, That, and the Other Thing* just showed up one day. Plans to include "This," "That," and the "Other Thing" sections with stories followed. For me, the title comes first, then the book. Voilà! The birth of another published book by RAMA!

Often, a flurry of story titles came to me like "This Isn't My First Rodeo," "This Little Piggy," and "This Is My Country." Soon, a dozen other titles were scribbled on my yellow legal pad. Yes, I'm old school. May there always be legal pads and fine ballpoint pens at the local Walmart!

Then "That Dog Won't Hunt," "That Don't Impress Me Much," and "My Nephew, Wayne" magically happened. Another five or ten "That" titles got a first draft.

The third section was a bit more challenging, but I focused on the word "thing." "Who Knew?" and "Everything Reminds Me About Something" were naturals. Each of the three book parts would include twenty or more stories and the length of the book would still be reasonable. I seldom buy a book with more than four hundred pages. I think having short chapters is also attractive to readers.

Quirky title? Yeah, but maybe intriguing enough that people will pick up and purchase. As with my other non-fiction writing, you'll find some politics, some religion, a little trivia, and a lot of baseball. Sorry, no pictures this time, but I think everyone will find some "things" of interest. And, if other "This," "That," and the "Other Thing" thoughts come to my readers in the middle of the night (or day), send them to me for a sequel. I'll give you credit for the story titles and will send you a free copy.

RAMA

The "This" Section

This Ain't My First Rodeo 5

This Little Piggy 7

This Is My Quest 11

This Is A Stickup! 13

Dissen 15

This Too Shall Pass 16

This Present Crisis 18

This Animal 21

This Is My Country 24

This Is Your Brain On Drugs 27

This Is Insane! 29

This I Know 32

This Is My Body, This Is My Blood 34

This Kind of Love 37

This Is the Feast of Victory 38

This Fellow Was With Him! 41

This Is the Day the Lord Has Made 43

This Is Most Certainly True 45

This Is the Word of the Lord 48

This Is the City 50

This Just In 52

This Is Your Captain Speaking 55

This Product Contains Peanuts 58

And So This Is Christmas 60

This Is the Life 64

This Day Give Us Bread 66

This Is the Gate of Heaven 69

This Ain't My First Rodeo

When I mention rodeo, what are the first thoughts that come to mind?

Roping? Bull riding (the hands down favorite event)? Barrel racing? Bronco-busting cowboys? Maybe bareback horse riding? Wrestling steers to the ground?

Rodeo is the state sport in Wyoming (nicknamed the Cowboy State), South Dakota, and Texas. In the Canadian province of Alberta and throughout the American west, rodeo is big!

"This ain't my first rodeo" is an idiom frequently heard today, usually used when a less experienced person tries to advise a more experienced person. The expression may have started with a country music artist (Vern Gosdin) who recorded a song by that title in 1990 (Columbia: Hank Cochran and Max D. Barnes).

Kristi Noem, the South Dakota governor, is a cowgirl, of sorts. And, I might add, a very attractive lady and politician, a rising star of the GOP. Noem participates in the great buffalo roundup each year at Custer State Park, many cowboys and cowgirls on the ride. The roundup draws thousands of spectators yearly.

The buffalo roundup is done on the 70,000-plus acres of the state park to check the health of the herd and cull the weak ones. The herd size varies with conditions, but each year includes more than 1,200 buffalo. Custer State Park is part of the Black Hills area, named after the Lieutenant Colonel George Armstrong Custer.

If Noem does become a candidate for the presidency of our country, the idiom that Gosdin sang about will likely be heard in her campaign for office. The speeches, photo ops, and public appearances would be many. Cowgirl hats could rival the Trump MAGA hats in our country for concerts, political conventions, and, of course, American rodeos.

This Little Piggy

Is there any parent or grandparent who has not used this nursery rhyme with their infant or toddler? At bedtime, bath time, or at any time, tugging lightly at each of the kid's toes, and saying:

"This little piggy went to market (big toe),
This little piggy stayed home (the long toe),
This little piggy had roast beef (the middle toe),
This little piggy had none (the fourth toe),
This little piggy cried, 'wee, wee, wee,' all the way home (pinky toe)."

When the littlest toe was pulled, to finish the rhyme and the bedtime fun, maybe a little tickle on the foot?

The title "This Little Piggy" first appeared in 1728 in "The Nurses Song." The full version appeared in 1760 in *The Famous Tommy Thumb's Little Story-Book*.[1] You can find different versions of the nursery rhyme, but the expression "little piggy" was not used until the mid-twentieth century.

What comes to your mind when you read or hear, "This Little Piggy?" I may be a bit quirky, but here are a few of my thoughts, the somethings that I am reminded about when hearing the rhyme.

1. This little piggy went to market

What? He went to the store? Why? To buy some corn, some vegetables, or fruit? To buy a nose ring? To meet some piggy friends?

I guess you could look at it differently, too. Went to market? What? To be sold and made into pork chops, pork butt, sausage, bacon, ribs, pork loin, or maybe an Easter ham? Such a trip to market would not be voluntary!

There's a saying among farmers when they butcher and pack the meat of a pig: "We use every part of the pig, including the squeal." Pig feet, pig tails, pig ears, pig intestines, pig skin, pig bones, and many more pig products.

At the house and farm buildings where I was born and raised, with the exception of chickens, we had more pigs that any other farm animal. The pig lot was a rather barren area around back of the feed mill that my dad owned and operated. When it rained, that pig lot was all mud, and a favorite pig playground. The large boars and sows made deep holes in the ground where they often rested. When Dad decided it was time, some were trucked-off to the stock market in St. Louis. Often, one or two were processed at our house, filling the basement freezer with food for the winter and spring.

2. This little piggy stayed home

At home, there is plenty to eat, a place to sleep, and shelter from any storm. Maybe this piggy is a mama's boy. Maybe the piggy was abused by the rest of the litter? Big pigs can be mean!

3. This little piggy had roast beef

I don't recall feeding our pigs any meat products, but pigs would eat just about anything. Corn was a favorite, of course. Very hard field corn on the cob was a treat. When sweet corn for human consumption was harvested, the husks and the corn cobs were thrown to the pigs. If there were any leftovers from our table, those were thrown to the pigs, too. This normally was over the fence down by the barn, just past the woodshed. So, roast beef was not out of the question.

4. This little piggy had none

Probably the runt of the litter; not fast enough to grab the choice foods thrown to the lot. This little guy had to deal with whatever was left after all others had eaten their fill. Poor little piggy!

5. This little piggy cried, "wee, wee, wee," all the way home

Maybe he didn't know how far he could go? The pig lot is fenced on all sides. Maybe he escaped the lot through a hole in the fence? Frightened in the big old world, perhaps he just ran to be running. Crybaby!

I hope my thoughts in this story were not too offensive to the readers. Oh, by the way, baby back ribs are favored by many of the barbeque crowd. Please know that baby back ribs have nothing to do with baby pigs.

FYI:

1. The top pork producing companies of the world include two from China, one from Thailand, one from the USA, and one from Brazil.

2. Top exporters of pork include the USA, Germany, Spain, Denmark, and Canada.

3. Top importers of pork include Japan, Italy, China, South Korea, and Germany.

4. Seventy percent of the "divine swine" is produced in five states of the USA: Iowa, Minnesota, North Carolina, Illinois, and Indiana.

5. A group of pigs is called a drove; sometimes a drift. I didn't know those terms. I bet you didn't either.

6. The pork industry of our country is more than a twenty-three billion dollar production; 26 percent of which is exported.

7. A female adult pig is called a sow. The male adult is a hog or boar. A baby pig is called a piglet. An average litter of piglets is seven or eight, but twelve to fourteen is not uncommon.

8. A story on pork would be remiss if there was no mention of SPAM. This pork product by Hormel has just five other ingredients: water, salt, potato starch, sugar, and sodium nitrite. Check the SPAM shelves at your grocery store to see numerous modern twists.

9. One more thing. Pigs smell! So, if raising pigs, you'll want to put them some distance from the house. A substantial fence is important because they can root-up a weak fence. And, speaking about rooting, pigs have a strong sense of smell. They are used to find and uproot truffles from soils near the roots of trees. Outside of Europe, truffles are rare. In the USA, some truffles can be found in Oregon, Tennessee, and North Carolina.[2]

This Is My Quest

quest: a long and arduous search for something[3]

I have many sleepless nights, but rather than getting an appointment with my PC or a specialist, I choose to make the diagnosis myself. I know the medical terms such as insomnia and apnea and I see the many commercial messages for such disorders. I'm told by some that I snore. I doubt that, though I've never stayed awake to know if that is true. And I'm not about to remedy the snoring with CPAP or other ways to prevent snoring.

When I see the suggestions for preventing sleeplessness, I'm dubious, as well. Change my sleeping position? I do that a half-dozen times a night! Lose weight? Yeah, right! Probably not going to happen! Avoid alcohol? Somehow, I thought that drinking brought on sleep. Anyway, I've cut down on alcohol significantly. Open nasal passages? I thank God regularly that this is not a problem. Taking six or more deep breaths through both nostrils and exhaling works wonders with that. Try it! Change pillows? I like Mike Lindell, but I've not ordered MyPillow. I do cherish my pillow, however, and take it with me when I travel. Stay hydrated? I'm doing much better with that. No sugar Powerade, Mio Lemonade, Cran-Cherry juice, or just ice water works for me.

So, on a recent sleepless struggle, the song from *Man of La Mancha* popped into my thoughts. So, in the morning and even before trying to sleep, I made a few notes from the lyrics of "The Impossible Dream" and this story was created. You thought I'd never get there, right?

Goals in life are important. You don't get very far without goals, but I think goals are a little different than quests. "To fight the unbeatable foe, to run where the brave do not go, to right the unrightable wrong, to try when your arms are too weary, to reach the unreachable star." Another level, right? And then, "to follow that star, no matter how hopeless, no matter how far."[4] Wow! Talk about reaching your full potential!

Losing five or ten pounds is an attainable goal. Mirrors, buying a new suit, or coming real close to asking the flight attendant for a seatbelt extender; all good motivators. Eliminating obesity, curing diabetes, resolving insulin resistance? Now we're talking quests!

Achieving world peace? Curing our most catastrophic disease? Proving that life exists on places other than our Earth? Answering, to everyone's satisfaction, the question of how life began on this terrestrial ball? Ditto!

The former governor of Arkansas, Mike Huckaby, advertised a product called Relaxium. I have come very close to ordering the stuff. It is said to be drug-free and not habit-forming, yet I wonder why you must take it every night.

Age? I know it is a factor. Never one to take a nap since about the age of five, I sometimes find myself falling asleep on the couch before going to bed. So, I ask myself, if I went to bed before falling asleep, would I fall asleep easily and not toss and turn? By taking a two-hour respite at 10:00 p.m., should I delay getting to bed until 2:00 a.m.? Should I train myself not to always get up in the morning by 6:00 a.m.? Governor, what was that Relaxium number again?

This Is A Stickup!

At first thought, this statement seems strange. Most of us may think it means that a crime is happening. It might be a robbery preceded by the threatening statement, "Okay, everybody, hands up!" At a jewelry store, at the gas station, or at a bank, those who plan a heist fully intend to get as much loot as they can. The shop owners and any unfortunate customers and employees have their hands in the air, phalanges pointing skyward like burnt branches and tree trunks after a raging wildfire.

Why the hands in the air? The armed robbers don't want anyone reaching for their cell phones or concealed weapons. Keep your hands where they can see them, right?

Armed robbery is a major problem in our country. It has been since the daily stagecoach from Laramie was stopped on a dusty trail by a half-dozen men with bandanas hitched up over their mouths and noses demanding the cash box to be thrown to the ground.

In some parts of our country, California particularly, one can get away without penalty if the stolen goods are less than $1,000 in value. Hard to believe? Yes, but apparently true. Elected judges and district attorneys actually tell that to the public! Are you kidding me?! Talk about being soft on crime! But then again, few, if any, persons who looted major merchandise in the street rioting and demonstrations of 2020 were ever apprehended, arrested, and penalized. So many anti-law policies following the George Floyd thing in Kenosha resulted in great laxity for criminal acts.

It has been many months now since the Waukesha, Wisconsin tragedy during the Christmas parade. In the streets of that small community near Milwaukee, the driver of a fast-moving vehicle killed six people and injured more than forty children, young people, and elderly as he tried to escape arrest and penalty. The driver had a rap sheet about as long as the parade route. He had been released on a bail bond for $1,000 just days before the carnage.

In a following story, a liberal U.S. congressman stated in an interview that all federal inmates should be released from their sentences as a matter of social justice. What foolish and dunderheaded officials we have in some parts of our country! And I feel really bad about taking a sample grape from the refrigerated case!

The Biden-Harris administration's policies at the Mexican-American border only added to the lawlessness at the moment and that to follow. What mayhem was to come from so many illegal immigrants entering our country, largely unvetted, flown to wherever they wanted to go at taxpayer's expense!

Hands up, America! This is a stickup!

Dissen

I've never delved into family ancestry. I leave that to my brother, Gilbert, who has done a lot for the rest of us. When people ask me about my name, Althage, I'm not certain about the history, so I'll say, "A lot of German, and maybe parts in the North." Someone told me that the translation is "old day," but I've never checked on that either.

There is a small community in Missouri called Dissen. I thought it was closer to where I grew-up (Franklin County), just west of St. Louis. But Dissen is in the bootheel of our state (Cape Girardeau County).

There is a city in Germany called Dissen. Settlers in the U.S. from that area apparently named their settlement in Missouri Dissen. I've not been to either of the two Dissens. Dissen, Missouri has its share of jokesters. An out-of-towner might tell you, "I've never been to Dissen, but I stopped at a diner in Datten last week for lunch."

Did you see that one (Datten) coming, and now know why this is a small story in my book? Dissen? This one. Datten? That one.

I probably owe this story to Uncle Virgil. He liked to use that joke in our family get-togethers. I'll need to ask other Kasmann relatives about "that one."

This Too Shall Pass

Are there events in your life that you are not real anxious to experience? You've noticed recently that your hips or knees ache after short walks or while you are on your feet at work. Your kids invite you to join them on an Orlando, Florida trip. Maybe go to one of the Disney parks or Universal Studios? Then you ask yourself, "Can I keep up with the kids and grandkids and enjoy Disney World, or would it be better to just stay home?"

The expression is said to be a Persian proverb, a truism, suggesting that life is made of little or passing moments, the temporary nature of our human existence. "This too shall pass" conjures-up some rather deep thinking.

Some say the expression may have had a biblical origin. First John 2:17 (NKJV), for example, "and the world is passing away, and the lust of it; but he who does the will of God abides forever." Or Matthew 24:35 (NKJV), "Heaven and earth will pass away, but My words will by no means pass away." Each of those New Testament writers reflect on what is lasting, which is the sinner is saved or rescued by the grace of God, resulting in salvation and eternal life.

As an aside, perhaps with no relevance at all to this story, I've made-up a couple of "food truisms," just for casual conversation. How about, "You cannot put too much salt on a baked potato." Or, "If you use honey on a muffin or biscuit on Sunday morning, you'll still have some honey on your wrist, hands, or mouth on Tuesday." Anyone agree with me on those?

Persian poets claim the expression began during the Middle Ages. It is sometimes found in wisdom literature across cultures in historical writings.

So, it's tax time for state and federal reports. You've had major damage to your house and property. Your wife has lost her job. Your two children need braces. As the filing dates approach, you ask yourself, "How will I resolve my family finances"? Then, come June, by some miracle, you are still afloat. Your spouse has gotten a new job, an even better one. The insurance payments were more than you expected. And the IRS has agreed to a schedule of tax payments that you can handle. Voilà! This too shall pass!

You're a single mom diagnosed with colon cancer six weeks ago. You've planned for the effect of chemo treatments. You've purchased two inexpensive wigs and made arrangements for the care of your two-year-old for two days a week. But it still seems like you'll never get through these hills and valleys. Your friends at work and your family are on your side and your pastor is your chief cheerleader. Voilà! You see some light after surgery and the end of chemo. You've learned to be thankful for every new day. Your child has no problem with the caretakers.

Each night, you look forward to the next day, and you trust God for your future.

This too shall pass!

This Present Crisis

crisis: a time of intense difficulty, trouble, or danger[5]

A crisis in the life of an individual or a family can pop up at any time. The short list could include major injury, loss of job, divorce, the death of a loved one, critical disease, and natural disasters (wild fires, severe weather, floods, earthquakes, etc.). These, more broadly, affect communities, cities, states, and nations, even the world. Pandemics come to mind.

For all of 2020 and much of the next two years, COVID-19 affected everyone everywhere.

In late 2021, the short list of crises in our country was not that short: chaos at our southern border, rising inflation, the remaining Americans and supporters of our country in Afghanistan, the constant threat of China, our growing national debt, and others. Some put climate change on that list or even at the top of the list. For me, climate change as a crisis comes just after measles, potato blight, frosts in Kansas, and ragweed allergies.

I'm reminded of the oft-heard comment by Rahm Emanuel, "You never want a serious crisis to go to waste."[6]

Other words for crisis, preferred by some, include calamity, catastrophe, and emergency, among others.

Sorry for the lengthy set-up for this story, but I thought it necessary for putting it in the "This" section of the book.

Just before Thanksgiving, the Jacob Blake affair in Kenosha, Wisconsin got the American people riled, like police shootings often do. The twenty-nine-year-old Black man was paralyzed from the waist down after four of seven shots entered his back while resisting arrest. A 911 phone call from Blake's girlfriend initiated the event. At the time, there was a warrant for Blake (sexual abuse, trespassing, and disorderly conduct). Blake had been tased before those shots were fired.

Major protests and violence in the streets resulted, causing unbelievable destruction of property in the center of Kenosha. The George Floyd riots and street violence had occurred two months earlier in Minneapolis.

In January 2021, Kenosha County prosecutor announced that the officer who fired the shots and others of the police force would not be charged, though they would be put on administrative leave. Three months later, the officer returned to duty on the police force.

Late in 2021, *This Present Crisis* by Michael Youssef was advertised on TV. His subtitle was, "Hope for This Present Crisis." That warranted this story in my book. Youssef offers his "Seven Steps Path to Restoring A World Gone Mad." In it, he delineated, "the only possible solution to current crises." In a religious perspective, he wrote that, "our country and the world must either unite around Jesus Christ or continue to attack and destroy "slowly descending into the abyss of chaos."[7]

Another name familiar to those who follow national news is Kyle Rittenhouse. I have no knowledge of Wisconsin law. Neither do I know anything about jury deliberation in the Rittenhouse case, charged with murdering two men, both white, and injuring a third, also white. Watching much of the live TV coverage, jury deliberation to begin in mid-November 2021, I see no way for Kyle Rittenhouse to be found guilty of the charges. Even Geraldo Rivera, often taking a more liberal stance, agrees with a probable "not guilty" outcome (CNN, WSNBC, ABC, CBS, other media to the contrary).

Police and authority in Kenosha, Chicago, and other cities were reported to have prepared for major protests and rioting again, even before the case was given to the jury. If there is an acquittal in the Rittenhouse case, the chaos will undoubtedly return. This present crisis will descend into the dark abyss!

FYI:

1. Some stories in my book were written at the time they were happening. When possible, I update the information once the story concludes.

2. In an 1845 poem, James Russell Lowell used a title similar to Youssef, written as a protest against the Mexican-American War. Decades later, it became the inspiration for the title of *The Crisis*, a magazine published by the NAACP.

3. With reference to the Rahm Emanuel quote (above), his explanation was that "a serious crisis is an opportunity to do things you thought you could not do before." More conservative politicians and talk show hosts tended to put their own interpretation on it.

4. Though acquitted on all charges late in 2021, on February 1, 2023, a federal judge allowed a lawsuit by the father of Anthony Huber, killed by Rittenhouse in Kenosha in 2020. So, the saga continues. Kyle Rittenhouse was found in Florida, where he has been an outspoken advocate for gun rights. He has a large following on Twitter. Stay tuned!

This Animal

When three of my grandkids were pre-teens, much of our time together was spent on the telephone. Occasionally, they visited me in New Orleans. At other times, I met them in Miami, Orlando, or on vacation at Sanibel Island. Our phone times tended to be lengthy because all three girls liked to play a guessing game that we called, "This Animal."

For example, this animal likes gardens and woodlands, would not win many races with other forest friends, even though this animal has four legs, and there's a chocolate-caramel treat named for them. If you guessed a turtle, you win. You get to quiz me now.

Kailyn, the oldest of the Miami triad, tried this one with me: This animal is quite small. It would fit easily in one hand, but you might not want to hold it. It is mostly black and yellow, maybe some small areas of white? Since I've been a gardener all of my life, I tried a few small creatures before asking, "Is it a bumblebee?" Of course, it was!

The "This Animal" game is really fun and can be played with any age group. Grandma and grandpa could enjoy it any time they were together. Teacher and students could have a great break from regular class work once a week or just for fifteen minutes. Vacations, trips in the car, camping times, a phone/Skype time would work well. It's always rewarding when you guess the animal and especially pleasing when you stump the other player(s).

This, That and the Other Thing

Try these two, hopefully to spur your interest in the simple game and maybe even challenge you to stump others for a little while. Answers later.

1. This animal is large and is considered dangerous by most people. He (She) likes a jungle environment, and, in some parts of the world, a grassland or savanna location. This animal is a predator and usually lives with other members of the family. Too easy?

2. This animal is about as ugly as an animal gets. It is an omnivore, meaning it eats both plants and animals (usually small ones like rodents, insects, etc.). They are native to the Americas, hunt for food at night, and are quite harmless to people.

Answers:

Number 1 is the lion, the second largest cat in the world, and cousin to leopards and jaguars. Lions live in a pride, which may have fifteen or more members. In sub-Saharan Africa, the zebra, wildebeest, and water buffalo are their chief prey. Lions live an average of ten to fourteen years, and mark their territory with their scent and lion's roar.

Number 2 is the opossum. In North America, we often omit the letter "o" and simply call them possums. In Australia, this animal is also known as a possum, one of several marsupials, native to the land down under. When threatened, possums often "play possum" as they pretend to be sick or even dead. Sometimes people "play possum," too. You?

The possibilities for the "This Animal" game are limitless. The millions of animal species in the world include six different kinds: mammals, birds, reptiles, amphibians, fish, and invertebrates.

While most of us can name only a handful of bee varieties, there are 20,000 varieties of bees in the world. Even the turtle varieties include 356 different ones.

Your turn. Quiz me! How about the emu, the turkey vulture, camel, Mississippi kite, or purple finch? The scorpion, the coral snake, hummingbird, earthworm, or bald eagle?

This Is My Country

"I pledge allegiance to the flag of the United States of America."

I have two questions for you:

1. In which of the four quadrants of the U.S. do (would) you prefer to live: North, South, East, or West?

2. If you could live in any other country of the world, which would be your top three choices?

Please make your choices before you read my choices.

Personally, I'd choose the southern quadrant. I have lived in seven different states. I'll put Missouri and Nebraska in the North, New York in the East, and Texas and Florida in the South. I have not lived in the western part of our country.

If I had to choose another part of the world, first I'd take a quiet village in Switzerland. Then a beautiful beach in Belize. Third, maybe one of the fifteen islands in the Seychelles, an archipelagic nation in the Indian Ocean at the eastern edge of the Somali Sea. Guess you could call me a Southerner, having lived in the South more than half of my life. New Orleans is real nice, if you choose a good neighborhood and don't mind the constant vigilance on the tropics, June through November. We call that the "cane" season.

I wonder if there are song titles that start with the words "this," "that," or "the other thing"? I found a couple for the "This" section of the book.

"This is My Country" by Vaughn Monroe was composed in 1940 (lyrics by Don Raye, music by AI Jacobs) and first recorded by Fred Waring and the Pennsylvanians in 1942. It was usually played at the end of the Disney World and Disneyland fireworks shows. With so much anti-American and anti-patriotic sentiment eight decades later, I'm not sure that it is still the case. One or two days at either Disney parks is more than enough for me in my latter life, but I'll always enjoy the song.

Here's the introductory verse of the song and the other verses:[8]

"What difference if I hail from North or South?
Or from the East or the West?
My heart is filled with love for all of these,
I only know I swell with pride
And deep within my heart
I thrill to see Old Glory paint the breeze."
"This is my country, land of my birth.
This is my country, grandest on earth.
I pledge thee my allegiance,
America to hold.
This is my country, to have and to hold."
"This is my country, land of my choice.
This is my country, hear my proud voice.
I pledge thee my allegiance,
American the bold,
To have and to hold,"
"With my hand upon my heat, I thank the Lord,
For all | love is here within her gates.
My soul is rooted deeply in the soil on which I stand,
For these are mine, my own United States."

How can one not proudly say, then; one nation, under God, with (no matter what some might say) liberty and justice for all!

This Is Your Brain On Drugs

In 1987, public service announcements (PSAs) regularly told us, more warned us, about the use of narcotics. The "Don't Do Drugs" campaign had different versions of the TV spot, one of them employing a fry pan and eggs. A fresh egg was dropped into a hot skillet. Then the egg was shown, fried to a crisp. The message: "This is your brain on drugs."

Some saw these PSAs as scare tactics. The egg industry didn't appreciate the use of their product, putting eggs in an inferior light.

Now, forty years later, we wonder if such anti-drug messages accomplished their objective? If you watch much TV, you know that the pharmaceutical manufacturers continue to push their medicines to reduce or eliminate your various pains and discomforts. The list of side effects for use of many of them is as scary as the problem they seek to prevent (thoughts of suicide and possible death sometimes included). In 2022, fentanyl, whether made in China, Mexico, or other locations, is a major scare for youth and adults. Other drugs and pills of every sort laced with a small amount of fentanyl can cause immediate death.

We see "brains on drugs" in our community every day. Visible examples of most young or middle-age males, in shabby dress, dirty face and hair, preaching, shouting-out, or talking to themselves, shaking their fists or fingers at someone, real or imagined. You feel sorry for these indigents, yet you choose to not confront them or help them. You wonder about the risks they took which resulted in their present state of mind? As cruel as it may be, seeing what drugs have done to them may be a far better prevention for you than any PSA or poster.

Talk about "poster children"!

This Is Insane!

These three words are so overused today! If one listens to a few hours of cable news today, you might hear the expression six or more times. The expression has become as trite as "I hear what you're saying" or "Tell me about it."

What is so insane? There are so many areas of our life today, so many contexts, that to mention all of them would be tedious. For starters, the soft-on-crime attorneys, judges, and public officials, the southern border crisis, the ever-increasing national debt, the socialist views on oil and gas production, inflation affecting food, travel, and basic human needs, drug trafficking, and human trafficking that is such a large part of the immigration problem.

You hear these three words in the field of sports, too. The MLB trade deadline is early August. Juan Soto turned down an insane offer of five hundred million dollars, hoping to get more from another team. A great hitter certainly, yet he, like all of the other baseball hitters, do well to hit safely in three of ten times at bat. Come-on man! Five hundred million dollars?! Insane!

The NCAA allows and supports a male swimmer to compete in female swim events. Transgendered or not, this should be a no-brainer! No! No! No! That's insane! Consider a few "what ifs" if such blind thinking continues in athletics:

1. A transgendered male wins every professional female golf tournament that he/she enters? Are there any women who don't mind a second place finish? The runner-up cash?

2. A transgendered male knocks the snot out of every female UFC contender, severely injuring most of the women he/she fights?

3. A transgendered male of superior height and offensive skills trounces all other women in women's basketball?

4. A transgendered male track star takes every gold medal in the next Olympics, soundly defeating women track stars from any and all countries?

Ridiculous! Unbelievable! Totally unfair! Insane might be closer to the appropriate exclamation, but even those seem trite at mid-year 2022.

In professional basketball and football, examples of insanity, both from the individual athlete perspective and that of the team owner, are many and varied. The Cleveland Browns of the NFL were newsworthy as training camps opened in 2022. Deshaun Watson was to be the starting quarterback, pending a judge's decision on the claims of two dozen women regarding Watson's personal conduct off the gridiron.

Judge Sue L. Robinson hit Watson with a six-game suspension to start the 2022 schedule. This was apparently based on twenty-three of twenty-four civil cases. The NFL Players Association said it would not appeal the judge's decision. Roger Goodell, the NFL commissioner, would have three days to decide any action he chose. Contrition of Watson's part never happened, maintaining his innocence. The number of personal conduct claims, by itself, was insane! No matter what Goodell decides, many sports writers predicted that Watson would practice with the team and take the field as quarterback for game seven.

Watson and other professional athletes may be the exception for character flaws. Domestic violence among certain NFL players seemed a regular occurrence.

If I was the field judge for game seven and Watson was to take the snap, I'd throw as many flags before that snap as I could push into my belt. This was (is) not a Justice Kavanaugh question!

Tennis anyone? Skiing? Bobsled? Javelin? Boxing, in any weight division?

This I Know

Christian moms and dads, grandparents, Sunday School teachers, and teachers of pre-school and K-2 children, upon seeing the title, likely think of the song, "Jesus Loves Me, This I Know."

How do they know? As the song continues, "for the Bible tells me so," yes, knowledge of the Bible and belief in God's Word is a given for their quick thinking. Regular worship, personal or group Bible Study, and an appreciation for Christian pastors, teachers, and schools are prerequisites for Bible trivia.

Baptism! Is there a more cherished title given than to be called a child of God? No matter what the age, as the kids' song assures, we are weak, poor, miserable sinners, but "He is strong." No doubt about it: Jesus loves me.

To put this knowledge into more adult terms, consider the Apostles Creed. First Article, "I believe in God the Father." Second Article, "I believe in Jesus Christ." Third Article: "I believe in the Holy Spirit."

Some words from Dr. Martin Luther's explanation of the Third Article: "I believe that I cannot by my own reason or strength believe but the Holy Spirit has called me by the Gospel, enlightened me with His gifts, sanctified and kept me in the true faith."

This I Know

The certainty of God's love and grace, the assurance of salvation, and the never doubted forgiveness of sins all are reinforced by this simple child's song.

This Is My Body, This Is My Blood

Jesus instituted Holy Communion, the Eucharist, as He had dinner (the Last Supper) with His disciples just prior to His crucifixion.

Our pastor uses the words of Jesus every Sunday in the preparation for the sacrament of the altar. "This is my body (the host or bread), given for you, for the forgiveness of sins. This is my blood (the wine), shed for you, for the forgiveness of sins" (Matt. 26:26-30).

I realize that it is quite a stretch connecting baseball with Holy Communion, but let me try. At Busch Stadium in St. Louis, the Cardinals played the Dodgers just before the All-Star Game, mid-July 2022.

As the batter came to the plate, the centerfield camera focused on the batter, the catcher, and the umpire, but in the background, advertisements could be seen which usually changed each inning or half inning. There were ads for grass seed, rental cars, the Dierbergs grocery chain, children's hospitals, and others.

One of the others said, "He Gets Us," which is for the website of the same name (hegetsus.com). The ad also said, "Text for prayer, connecting with others." It was started by a group of people passionate about the authentic Jesus of the Bible. Part of the ad you could see had the words, "Jesus forgave errors." Baseball errors? Sins?

In Christian worship, and especially in Holy Communion, we confess that we make lots of errors in life, admitting that we are poor, miserable sinners in need of God's grace, love, and forgiveness.

For those readers who are not into baseball, an error is the misplaying of a ball which allows a batter or a base runner to advance one or more bases. While there are baseball games where no errors are committed by either team, it is somewhat common to see a game when one or more errors are made, some of which are responsible for one or more runs scored by the opponent.

The "He Gets Us" ad has been used in other venues. For example, at the 2022 Super Bowl game, the ad was run once in the first half and once in the second half.

Holy Communion practices vary among Christian churches. In my church as a kid in 1950s, we had Holy Communion once a month. Members would announce their intention to take communion for the following Sunday, both to assist with planning the elements (bread and wine) and to comply with church traditions. Many Christian churches today have Holy Communion in every worship service. Some churches do not have Holy Communion at all or offer the sacrament only rarely.

Jesus said, "Do this to remember Me." In my church today, it's hard to forget Jesus because our pastor uses His name in his sermons dozens of times in every worship. I wonder at times, is remembering Jesus the best test for determining real Christian worship? And for determining a real gospel message in the pastor's sermon?

In the garden, Eve took of the forbidden fruit, gave it to Adam, and he followed suit. When God asked about their error, Adam blamed Eve, and Eve blamed the serpent. Miserable mistakes, for sure, but God "got" Eve and Adam, too. A curse is put on the serpent when God spoke directly: "I will put enmity between you and the woman, and between your seed and her seed..." and the penalty for both followed. So, in the beginning, God's grace, love, and mercy resolved the circumstance (see Genesis 15 NIV).

God's pronouncement of the Savior was made just before man and woman were sent from the garden. Those sentences for error still apply today for all mankind. Yes, salvation is for all who believe. Forgiveness is for all who confess and believe. God's promise of eternal life is ours because He gets us!

This Kind of Love

Occasionally, I get ideas for book titles and/or stories from worship experiences. That was the case on November 7, 2021, our observance of All Saints Day.

I believe that my father and mother, my uncles and aunts, my sisters and brothers, my wife and I, and many other family and friends were (are) sinners. But I also believe that they were (are) saints. Not because of anything they or we have done or will do to earn that churchy title. We can think of ourselves as saints solely by God's grace and the sacrifice of Jesus at Calvary, His resurrection and victory over sin, death, and the devil. I believe that we will unite as children of God in heaven. Eternal life with God is ours because of God's love for us.

The epistle lesson for All Saints Day was from 1 John 3:1-3 (ESV): "See what kind of love the Father has given to us, that we should be called children of God, and so we are." I'll let you read the rest of that scripture in your Bibles. That kind of love for me and for you is the reason I wanted this scripture in the book. "And so we are" would make a wonderful t-shirt message. So, when someone asks, "You are what?" The easy answer is, "I am a child of God."

Enjoy your childhood! Remember the regard Jesus had for little children. Jesus was a little child.

He gets us!

This Is the Feast of Victory

This is a story about worship. It is also a story about change.

Most of us are familiar with the expression, "Time changes things." When my wife died, now more than twelve years ago, one of the ladies who called to console me said that to me. She was right, of course, Yet change is sometimes slow.

Sometimes people are happy (content) with things just as they are. But, in order to change things from "satisfied with life" to "something better in life," things must change. Henry Ford said, "If I asked my customers what they wanted, they'd have said," Don't change anything." Henry Ford wisely did not adopt that business practice.[9]

Change does not come without someone proposing something new or different. It does or often does not occur without problems. Woodrow Wilson said, "If you want to make enemies, try to change something." Remember when Coca-Cola changed their soft drink?

A quote from Mother Teresa speaks to the process of change: "I alone cannot change the world, but I can cast a stone across the waters to create many ripples."[10] And Harriet Tubman, the American political activist and abolitionist of our Civil War years followed with, "Every great dream begins with a dreamer. Always remember, you have within you the strength, the patience, and the passion to reach for the stars, to change the world."

Now, to the general topic of worship in Christian churches. There's no doubt that change in the church does not happen overnight. Most Christian churches of some size have committees or boards who study proposals and may recommend changes to the church-at-large. Language is often the case.

As a kid in Missouri in teenage confirmation class, when talking about final judgment (heaven or hell) and creedal change (Apostles Creed, Nicene Creed), the words were "to judge the quick and the dead." I wonder how long it took the church to change the word "quick" to "the living"?

The topic of church hymnals is a good one. I think my church presently has three approved hymnals. The one we use and the one perhaps most used in our congregations is *Lutheran Service Book*.[11] (The Commission on Worship of the LC-MS, 2006, Concordia Publishing House, St. Louis, Missouri). There are five "Orders of Worship," each of which might be used from time to time. Two of those include, as part of the liturgy, replacing the Kyrie with "This is the Feast of Victory (for Our God)," based on Revelation 5 and 19, selected verses. If you sang the Kyrie every Sunday and for special seasonal services for fifty years, perhaps 3,000 times, it took a few months to get familiar with the new "This is the Feast."

Both orders of service included the usual: invocation, confession, and absolution, the Bible readings (Old Testament, Epistle, and Gospel), the creed, the sermon, the prayers, the Lord's Prayer, four or more hymns, and the Benediction. Holy Communion is part of nearly every service in my church, emphasizing the importance of the sacrament. Many churches of other denominations celebrate the Lord's Supper much less often.

The feast? Well, it's not like the historical one at Plymouth with the Pilgrims in 1621. It's not like the ones we plan and enjoy each November with turkey, dressing, green bean casserole, and cranberry sauce. Actually, it's much better. This feast of victory is to the Lamb, to God, to Jesus!

"In a loud voice, they (thousands of angels) were saying, 'Worthy is the Lamb who was slain, to receive power and wealth and wisdom and strength and honor and glory and praise!'" Revelation 5:12 (NIV)

"Then a voice came from the throne, saying: "Praise our God all you His servants, you who fear Him, both great and small!' Then I heard what sounded like a great multitude, like the roar of rushing waters and like loud peals of thunder, shouting: 'Halleluiah!" Revelation 19:5-7 (NIV)

For our God Almighty reigns. Let us rejoice and be glad and give Him glory! We all have our favorite Christmas hymns. Is there any better Christmas music than Handel's "Halleluiah Chorus"? Maybe we should agree to a top five Christmas songs for worship. That process would create a real ruckus, right? Top ten? Top twelve?

This Fellow Was With Him!

If you ask ten people who were even remotely religious, "How many disciples did Jesus have?" you'd likely get many correct answers: twelve. Ask the same ten to name all twelve of them, you'd likely get few, if any, to name all twelve.

Among those disciples, most named would be Simon Peter, James, John, and perhaps Judas. This story is about Peter, the fellow who was with Jesus right to the end.

The passion of Christ, recorded in all four of the Gospels, is the substitutional atonement for our sins by Jesus on the cross of Calvary. It is the crucifixion of Christ.

Simon Peter! Is there a better example of a follower of Christ, yet also one who, when push comes to shove, would never deny his relationship with Jesus. "'Even if I have to die with you, I will never disown you.' And all the other disciples said the same" (Matt. 26:35).

Matthew recorded the prediction of Jesus that His disciples would abandon Him. "Then Jesus told them, 'This very night you will all fall away on account of me'" (Matt. 26:31).

Simon Peter was sitting in a courtyard when a servant girl declared, "This man was also with Jesus of Galilee." Peter responded with, "I don't know what you are talking about." Sounds like what a witness anywhere in the USA would say today.

At the gateway of the courtyard, another girl saw him and told the people who had gathered, "He was with Jesus of Nazareth." And, with an oath, Peter said, "I don't know the man!"

Peter's accent apparently gave him away. Those standing nearby said, "Surely you are one of them." A third time, Peter denied knowing Jesus. At that exact moment, a rooster crowed, and Peter recalled what Jesus had said. Scripture tells us that Peter went out and cried bitterly (Matt. 26:69-75).

When women (Mary Magdalene, Joanna, Mary, the mother of James, and others) went to the grave and discovered that Jesus had risen like He foretold, they hurried to tell the disciples (see Luke 24:9). Most of the twelve, minus Judas Iscariot, regarded the report as nonsense. "Peter, however, got up and ran to the tomb" (Luke 24:12). Not long after, Jesus appeared on numerous occasions.

Bold, brash, and a bit of a bully, Peter was a lot like us. On special occasions in the church (baptisms, confirmations, weddings, funerals, Easter, Christmas), it's easy to profess our faith and loyalty to Jesus. But in the garden, at the gate, at the trial of Jesus, and in many situations and circumstances in life today, it's easy to deny our Lord. That's what confession is all about. Thank God! He forgives!

Note: All Bible references are from the New International Version, 1978, and 1984. International Bible Society, 1973.

This Is the Day the Lord Has Made

As a teacher and an administrator in elementary Christian schools, I regularly led chapel services for the kids. Almost always, there were two groups: nursery through kindergarten, and elementary. The songs we sang were simple melodies with Christian messages. The one below you can even sing to start your day:

"This is the day (repeat)
That the Lord has made (repeat)
We will rejoice (repeat)
and be glad in it (repeat)
This is the day that the Lord has made (repeat)
We will rejoice and be glad in it (repeat)
This the day that the Lord has made"

The song is based on Psalm 18:24.

The COVID years were difficult for everyone. Everyone in the world! The outbreak of the virus, originating in Wuhan, China, changed our lives in churches, schools, entertainment, businesses both large and small, shopping, banking, exercising, and more.

I started writing and publishing books after retiring from forty-five years in Christian education. My wife died in 2010; the writing regimen was a great help to me. In the next two books, I tried to relate how COVID affected me, believing that it had similar effects on everyone else.

The first of the two was titled *This Is the Day the Lord Has Made*. The publisher did not want to confuse the two books for those ordering them, so the second book needed a slightly different title. The second book was then titled *This Is STILL the Day the Lord Has Made*. I strived to make the point that every day is a day that God has granted new life. COVID or not, that's a pretty good way to approach life. I did not contract the virus in those two years, but the pandemic certainly affected my faith and church life. Now, nearly four years later, it STILL does. Rejoicing isn't as easy and automatic as it once was. I recognize my sinful and selfish stance in the matter.

It would be interesting for me to know how COVID changed your life, for the good, the bad, or even the ugly (sinful). Confession is good for the soul!

This Is Most Certainly True

Any serious Lutheran catechumen will recognize this story title!

A catechumen is a student of the catechism. While these are most often the church's youth, there are also adult catechumens. A catechism is a book of questions and answers, used for religious instruction.

Lutheran? One of several Protestant religions, resultant from the reformation of the early sixteenth century, named for Martin Luther, the principal spokesman in the break with the Roman Catholic religion. Luther believed what he wrote and taught. That's why he used the superlative (most) in the expression.

A German monk, priest, and professor of theology, along with other reformers like Jan Hus and John Wycliffe, Luther was a central figure in the Protestant Reformation. His *Small Catechism* was written in 1529, a summary of Christian teaching (doctrine). He also wrote a *Large Catechism*. You can also find his lengthy exposition *A Preface to the Small Catechism*, in which he expresses his devotion to the truth of Scripture.

Martin Luther saw first-hand how deplorable conditions were as he visited the parishes of the Catholic church. He observed that the pastors of the church were incompetent as they were nearly unable to teach what the Scriptures actually said. The pastors' understanding of The Lord's Prayer, the Ten Commandments, and the Apostles Creed cause him to write a brief questions-and-answers book in plain and simple form. His *Small Catechism* centered on the six chief parts of instruction: The Ten Commandments, the Apostles Creed, the Lord's Prayer, the Sacrament of Holy Baptism, the Sacrament of the Altar (Holy Communion), and the Office of the Keys and Confession.

At the time, Charles V was the Roman Emperor and Leo X was the pope. The Catholic church leadership reacted swiftly once Luther posted his *Ninety-Five Theses* on the door of the church at Wittenberg. Luther was asked to retract his teachings and writings, but at the Diet of Worms (1521), Luther adamantly refused to retract anything. For his stance, he was excommunicated from the church and regarded as an outlaw by the emperor.

Several versions of the movie *Martin Luther* were made with the Diet (Court) of Worms being the most dramatic scene. Risking his life and limb, Luther's "Here I Stand" speech is regarded as a "best ever" statement of individual belief and freedom. It was delivered first in German and then in Latin, April 18, 1521. The speech concludes,

"If I am not convinced by proof of Holy Scripture, or by cogent reasons, If I am not satisfied by the text l have cited, and if my judgment ... I neither can nor will I retract anything, for it cannot be either safe or honest for a Christian to speak against his conscience, Here I stand. I cannot do otherwise. God help me."[12]

Charles V, at first, refused to arrest Luther, but on May 25, 1521, the emperor issued the Edict of Worms, charging Him with heresy and branding him a notorious heretic. Luther escaped to the Wartburg Castle, aided by friends and soldiers of the Elector of Saxony Fredrick ll. In June of that year, Luther married Katharina. Six children were born to the Luthers, three boys and three girls, several of which died at a young age.

This church history begs the question: What does the church believe today? Getting responses from one hundred Christians from the various Christian religions might reveal similar finds to what Luther discovered centuries ago.

There were many false teachers in the early Christian church. The creeds of the church were written in response to those falsehoods. The three most common creeds, though there were many others, are the Apostles Creed (AD 140-175), the Nicene Creed (AD 325-381), and the Athanasian Creed (AD 282-542). The Athanasian Creed sought to clarify the nature of the Holy Trinity. It is the longest of the three, used mostly on Trinity Sunday. The Apostles Creed was not authored by the apostles of Jesus, but it did reflect their teachings.

This entry in the book was written a few days after Thanksgiving 2021. I had leftover Christmas signs following a garage sale at my church (Peace of Earth, Joy to the World, Christmas Tree Farm, etc.). I offered the signs to my family who I had spent a wonderful Thanksgiving with. My daughter chose a really nice four foot sign that simply said, "I Believe." In her mind and in mine, it had nothing to do with Santa! True! Most certainly true!

Martin Luther a GOAT? Few would argue the inquiry, the "Here I Stand" defense and delivery being so poignant and memorable.

Anyone out there have Peyton Manning on speed dial? We Lutherans need to rally for the cause!

This Is the Word of the Lord

I don't visit many churches other than those "back home" and a few where my family worships. But, in those, and I suspect, in most churches, Bible readings are part of the service. An Old Testament reading, an Epistle from the New Testament, and a Gospel reading precede the sermon. The confession and absolution are also part of the early liturgy.

In the service book my church now uses, after the Old and New Testament readings, the pastor says, "This is the word of the Lord," and the congregation responds with, "Thanks be to God."

When I added this story to the "This" section, I wondered if this had always been a Lutheran thing or if it was a more recent addition, maybe initiated with the introduction of a new hymnal. I did not do any further research. My pastor was not sure either.

As a kid in church, and later as an adult, we learned about the three means of God's grace: Holy Baptism, Holy Communion, and the Word of God. In each of these, the Holy Spirit becomes part of our life. The Holy Spirit? Yes, the Lord and Giver of life, as we confess in the Nicene Creed.

Is there a most important Word of God for Christians. You'd have a difficult time choosing or naming just one among the many favorites. I'll cite a few, each from the Holy Bible New International Version (International Bible Society, 1973, 1978, and 1984):

Matthew 6:33–But seek first his kingdom and his righteousness...

Matthew 28:19–Therefore go and make disciples of all nations...

Luke 2 (and others)–the Christmas account

John 3:16–For God so loved the world...

John 13:34–Love one another...

John 14:6–"I am the way and the truth and the life...

Romans 8:38-39–[nothing] will be able to separate us from the love of God...

Ephesians 2:8–by grace you have been saved, through faith...

1 Peter 5:7–Cast all your anxiety on him because he cares for you.

Psalm 23:1–The Lord is my shepherd...

Put into a more general sense, we can be thankful for every word of the Lord!

Question: If you were asked, "What is the Bible about?" what would YOU say? My simple reply: The Bible is about God. It is about Jesus! So, each time the Bible is read, we reply with thanksgiving, "Thanks be to God, for Jesus!"

If your church is about Jesus, Him crucified, dead, buried, and risen for our salvation, then it is Thanksgiving every Lord's day. Thanks be to God who gives us the victory through our Lord and Savior, Jesus Christ!

This Is the City

How could I not include this one? Do you remember the unforgettable musical intro and theme of *Dragnet*, the half-hour crime drama on black-and-white TV (1951-1959), composed by Water Shuman? The characters and the memorable lines used in the production are also itched in our minds such as "This is the city, Los Angeles, California. I work here. I'm a cop," or, "The story you are about to see is true. The names have been changed to protect the innocent,"[13] from the chief actors Sergeant Joe Friday (Jack Webb) and officer Frank Smith (Ben Alexander).

Joe Friday was a no-nonsense, straight arrow detective, who always got his man/woman. "Just the facts, ma'am; just the facts. We were working the day watch out of homicide." The series had 276 episodes. If these were on TV today (and I guess one can find them), there would be a great following. People like police stories.

Jack Webb, also the producer of the show, did not lack for crime stories in Los Angeles in the 1950s, but what he had then for script writers does not compare with Los Angeles crime in 2022. Other big cities with violent crime today such as San Francisco, Seattle, Chicago, Philadelphia, Washington, D.C., New York City, and others are regulars on TV news shows.

Smaller metropolitan areas fare no better in crime statistics. In mid-summer of 2022, five lesser cities with the most murders per capita included New Orleans, Baltimore, Birmingham, St. Louis, and Milwaukee.[14]

So, what are the causes of criminal chaos in our country today? And were they the same as seventy years ago? In my opinion, the causes are quite different. Poverty, inferior education, the lack of job skills, dysfunctional families, and other causes may not be much different than now, but in 1950, law and order was the rule! Police were respected. In some sense, police were feared, in a good way. When the siren sounded and you saw those red and blue lights in your rearview mirror, you pulled over rather than trying to escape the law.

Defunding the police, hating the police, and disrespecting the police often seems the case today. Soft-on-crime policies by judges, district attorneys, and state attorneys today make criminals bold and combative. Failure to prosecute lesser crimes and serious felonies and no bail release simply return the offenders to the community. Other stories in this book speak to that trend.

At the end of *Dragnet* episodes, viewers were told about the charges brought against those arrested. A concluding comment simply stated, "In a moment, the results of that trial."

In the 50s, somehow you felt good, safer in your home and neighborhood, as you retired for the day. You might not have even locked your door, but leave your house, car, or truck unsecured, in any kind of community today, "Dumb, da dumb, dumb!"

This Just In

While watching cable news channels, all of them competing for audience, it is not uncommon to see, slashing across the screen, "Breaking News." While covering a story, one that will have "legs" (a story that will not go away soon), the reporter(s) will relate something new that has just happened, some new twist or circumstance that the producers think is significant enough to interrupt the present coverage or, at least, to put first on their telecast. A similar expression often used is, "This just in."

The folks in the South Gulf want all of the information they can get during the tropical storm season, June 1 through November 30. A storm whose status is upgraded from tropical storm to hurricane status (75 miles per hour sustained winds or greater) will quickly grab the attention of homeowners and business people. If the storm track and the "cone of influence" is forecast in their area, it may mean a need to batten down the hatches, check on evacuation routes, and plan for the potential dangers of such wind and rain storms.

Surprisingly, the 2022 hurricane season has been quite quiet. The season for tropical storms peaks in mid-September, so we in the New Orleans area are on a downward trend. We could still have plenty of activity in the final eighty days of the season, though. Everyone in our area and in Miami, Tampa Bay, Lake Charles, and Southeast Texas hopes that there will be no "This just in" interruptions in our TV viewing and daily lives.

This Just In

Stories about missing children and kidnapping are fairly common in 2022. For those personally affected, friends and family check constantly for new information. If a body has been found and a police news conference is to be held, they are all ears.

A train derailment, an earthquake, a wild fire threat, or other natural disaster/accident may each result in an interruption of local programming.

In mid-September 2022, the mid-term elections in our country are just seven weeks away. Elections for governors, senators, or representatives are followed closely. "This just in" on the TV is about as common as red beans and rice on Mondays.

The state of Pennsylvania is one such state, specifically for the senate race; John Fetterman versus Dr. Oz. Until recently, Democrat Fetterman had not agreed to debating the issue with his Republican counterpart, but being pressured to have one or more debates, Fetterman ultimately said he'd have just one.

Dr. Oz, the Republican National Committee, and perhaps many in Pennsylvania said, "Whoa! Debate?" With early voting set to begin in a few days, the sentiment was, "No way!"

Fetterman suffered a stroke, causing some speech and public language problems which kept him from appearances. He was regarded as an extreme liberal while Oz was regarded, by some, as an extreme conservative. Joe Biden said that such Republican candidate were a threat to our country. What a clown, our president.

Pollsters had the election as very tight, saying that the debate performances might be the deciding factor? If Fetterman decided to debate more than once, TV producers would interrupt local programming to announce the dates, locations, and times.

Only one debate was held. Fetterman's performance was one of the worst in our political history. To me, the man looks like a slob. His usual dress is sweatpants and a hoodie. Just the man I'd want to represent me in the U.S. Senate!

An update (following the elections):

Dr. Oz lost his bid for the U.S. Senate. John Fetterman joined the congress in January 2023. OMG! And this just in, in February 2023, John Fetterman entered a hospital for stroke complications and severe depression. As of March 1, it was undetermined as to when he might serve the people of Pennsylvania.

The 2022 hurricane season in the Atlantic included Fiona, particularly causing fatalities and damage in Puerto Rico, and Ian, which crossed Western Cuba and came onshore near Ft. Meyer's western coast. Ian crossed the state and went back into the Atlantic, with 114 reported deaths and major damage to Southwest Florida.

There were six storms that were named following Ian, only two of which had near hurricane winds of 70 to 75 knots. The fourteen named Atlantic storms was exactly average for a storm season. The average per season for major hurricanes is 3.2. The estimate for hurricane damage in 2022 was fifty-four billion dollars. Three hundred and thirty-seven deaths were caused by the fourteen named storms.

This Is Your Captain Speaking

The last time I flew anywhere was about six months ago, a trip to Miami for my granddaughter's high school graduation. There was a time in my life when I flew a lot. My wife worked for numerous airlines (Texas International, Continental, Southwest) when our children were young.

The perks for airline employees then were such that Barbara could get tickets (mostly standby) nearly any time she (we) wanted. Once, we saw an ad for a hamburger joint (Fuddruckers), the closest restaurant being in San Antonio. The five of us packed a short bag of necessities and we flew from New Orleans to central Texas just to try the burger. On another occasion, a friend at church offered me (us) tickets to an LSU game at Colorado. Barbara and I packed up, went for Saturday's game in Boulder, and stayed the night.

In my search for another story or two for the "This" section of the book, I came up with the title for this one: "This Is Your Captain Speaking." I don't think I've heard that announcement from the cockpit in many other flights, but I think I actually heard these words at least once waiting for takeoff. Sometimes the captain made the announcement because of a delay in takeoff, a kind of apology from the airline.

There were other announcements from the captain back then such as, "Ladies and gentlemen, those lights off to our left are the lights of Wrigley Field. The

Cubs play the Cardinals tonight," or, "If you wonder what the bright lights off to our right might be, that's the Las Vegas strip coming up."

Most of the communication from the crew now are made by the attendants. "The captain has turned-on the fasten your seatbelts sign. We expect some bumpy weather for the next ten minutes, so please stay seated."

All airlines still use the pre-flight instructions about seatbelts, flotation devices, plane exits, and oxygen masks. These are mostly ignored by many passengers today for such things are rarely used or needed, but it is always good to be safe.

Hijacking aircraft was a hot topic for a while, but the employment of air marshals on flights eased that concern for passengers. The last hijacking of an airplane that most Americans remember would be the 9/11 terrorists on several flights. Those resulted in the deaths of nearly three thousand people and the destruction of the World Trade Center towers in New York City.

On that fateful day, four planes were involved, nineteen hijackers in total. The commercial airplanes were flown into each of the towers, another into the Pentagon near Washington, D. C., and the fourth into a field in Pennsylvania.

A statistic which I found amazing is that only 5 percent of the world's population has ever been on a plane. And, not so surprising, 80 percent of the folks in the U.S. have had one or more flights. In a 24-hour day, there are 8,000 planes in the air at any one time, 5,000 of those in our country.[15]

In writing about airplanes and air travel in previous books, I commented more than once that the 1903 flight by the Wright brothers at Kitty Hawk went no farther than the length of one of the modern passenger planes. Air speed of that historic flight was about thirty miles per hour. Modern jet aircraft, once cruising speed is accomplished, fly at 500 or more miles per hour.

You might find this research a bit interesting. Hijacking planes started as early as 1919, involved a great variety of aircraft, both large and small, and in parts of the world that may not have made news in the U.S. Some of those did not involve casualties. Unfortunately, some did.

This Product Contains Peanuts

If you refuel at self-service gas pumps, you have seen the sign "Contains 10 percent ethanol." This additive is not as new as you might think. Sometimes ethanol goes by other names: ethyl alcohol, grain alcohol, gasohol, or E10. These are organic chemical compounds, naturally produced by fermentation of sugars by yeasts.

When shopping for maple syrup or other pancake or waffle syrups, many look for a syrup that does not contain high fructose corn syrup. Of the many products on the grocery shelf, very few indicate "no high fructose corn syrup."

Another food product that many individuals and families take seriously is the peanut and/or other tree nut warning. Reactions to peanuts and tree nuts can be horrific. I'm currently reading a book by Adrian McKinty called *The Chain* by Mulholland Books (Little, Brown and Company). A young girl, kidnapped and held under very unusual circumstances, has a severe reaction to Rice Krispies, which, in small print, indicates the product may have "traces of nuts." Until the brother and sister holding the young girl can find with an EpiPen, the description of her condition is more than scary.

I recall *The Big Bang Theory* season one, episode sixteen ("The Peanut Reaction") when Howard Wolowitz is taken to the hospital after a reaction to eating peanuts. His swollen face was difficult to watch until resolved by the nurses. Kudos to the make-up department of the popular show!

Hundreds of foods can cause serious allergic reactions (anaphylaxis) to peanuts and tree nuts (e.g., cookies, pastry, ice cream, cereals, breads, salads, sauces, etc.). Unless resolved, the anaphylaxis can be life-threatening. Close to four million people in the U.S. are or need to be cautious about foods even with small traces of nuts. Even lotions, shampoos, and pet foods can contain traces of tree nuts.

Sometimes you feel like a nut. Sometimes you don't. That's the Mounds and Almond Joy jingle. Those allergic to nuts are super careful not to eat any foods or use any products that could cause minor or major reactions.

FYI:[16]

1. Brazil, producing ethanol from sugar cane, leads the world in ethanol production.
2. The U.S. produces ethanol from corn. Iowa, Nebraska, and North Dakota produce the greatest amounts. Iowa produced nearly five billion gallons in 2020.
3. Ethanol used as fuel dates back to the Henry Ford era (1890s). The Model T ran on gasoline, ethanol, or combination of the two.

And So This Is Christmas

Ask one hundred people, "What is your favorite holiday of the year?" Christmas is most likely number one, right? Thanksgiving maybe number two? Also on the short list might be Independence Day, Halloween, Memorial Day, or Labor Day?

Let's just stay with Christmas for this "This" story.

Ask one hundred people, "What is your favorite Christmas song?" Now, the response would be many and varied. Many will name a Christmas carol. Many will name non-religious songs and others will choose religious songs. The long list would contain "Jingle Bells," "Frosty the Snowman," "I Saw Mommy Kissing Santa Claus," "Joy to the World," "Silent Night," and "We Three Kings" to name only a few.

There's a Christmas song that would certainly not make my top ten, and one which would likely not be on most personal top lists. That's the title of this story and Christmas song: "And So This is Christmas."

I'm sure there is more history and information about this song than what I am using. I just like the melody. John Lennon, Celine Dion, and others have recorded the song. I prefer the Celine Dion version,[17] but the lyrics are quite the same. Here are the lyrics in the early part of the song:

And So This Is Christmas

"So this is Christmas
And what have you done?
Another year over
And a new one just begun.
And so this is Christmas
I hope you have fun
The near and the dear one
The old and the young.
A very merry Christmas
And a happy new year
Let's hope it's a good one
Without any fears."

Later in the lyrics, fighting and wars are hinted along with other things that are wrong in the world (e.g., poverty, injustice, racial conflict, etc.). I don't like those things, and I suppose you don't either, but, again, I just like the song!

Here's another that I like that may not be on your list. "Pretty Paper" (1963, written by Willie Nelson, first recorded by Roy Orbison and later by Nelson). Like many favorite songs, "Pretty Paper" has an interesting origin. Nelson recalled seeing a handicapped man selling pencils and paper on the street during the Christmas season.

Elvis Presley's "Blue Christmas" (1957) won't be on many favorites list, but the truth is that many people do not have a joyous Christmas. Some don't have a white Christmas. Some Christmases for some folks are pretty "blue."

"If We Make It Through December" (1973) by Merle Haggard, my favorite country singer. Okay, to be so negative, but there are reasons I like the song, thinking back to the passing of my wife from breast cancer in early January a dozen years ago.

"I'll Be Home For Christmas" (1943) by the Oak Ridge Boys, but originally Bing Crosby, Frank Sinatra, and others. Does that one make your list?

"Have Yourself a Merry Little Christmas" by Carrie Underwood. Judy Garland sang it in the *Meet Me in St. Louis* movie. "Christmas In Dixie" (1982) by Alabama. "Santa Looked A Lot Like Daddy? (1970) by Buck Owens.

And, how about this one? "Grandma Got Run Over By A Reindeer" is a Christmas song that you just have to sing along to once you've heard it. Well, this one caused me to write a Christmas song about Grandpa, as I tried to use the same meter/melody. Sorry to my liberal friends around the country, but politics had entered my thoughts while writing and attempting some rhyme:

Grandpa Got So Buzzed

"Grandpa got so buzzed when he drank whiskey,
 I decided that I'd write a country song,
 Bars, beer, booze, and yes, a few wild cowboys,
 Someone's got to right the nation's wrongs!"

"Right now the big problem is inflation,
 For most of us daily there is pain.
 The cost of everything just keeps on soaring,
 Brown and blue eyes crying in the rain."

"There's always problems at our southern border.
 Since Trump left us the place has gone to hell.
 Women, men, and even little babies cross the river.
 Our best and wisest leaders say, 'Oh, well!'"

"In cities large and small, big crime is raging,
 Criminals and crooks of every kind,

Take what they want when they can get it,
No prison, community service, and not fined."

"Some Dems think they've found gold with Roe v. Wade,
Come November you just wait and see.
May better heads prevail in our elections,
Life, liberty, and joy for you and me."

Don't look for this one on anyone's Christmas top ten!

This Is the Life

What comes to mind when you think about religious broadcasting?

Sunday morning worship broadcasts of local church services?

"Zoomed" worship services for shut-ins, also popular during the COVID-19 pandemic?

TV specials, especially at Easter and Christmas?

Evangelists who had a following at one time, but were disgraced because of personal errors? Jimmy Swaggart? Jim Bakker? Robert Tilton?

Popular preachers with large TV audiences, past or present? Billy Graham? Franklin Graham? T.D. Jakes? Joel Osteen?

Other evangelists, preachers, or Bible study teachers like Dwight Moody, Charles Stanley, John Hagee, Jerry Falwell, or David Jeremiah?

It is rare to find a long-running television anthology with a religious format. For Lutherans like me, *This is the Life* was such a program, produced by the Lutheran Church-Missouri Synod and distributed by the International Lutheran Laymen's League (1952-1988). This half-hour show was based on the Fisher family; father, mother, and three children, two teens and a ten-year-old. The focus was on every day, contemporary problems that were always resolved with Christian solutions. Topics centered on morality, infidelity, drug use and abuse, juvenile issues, bigotry, racism, censorship, and more. Pastor Martin had a usual role, the pastor at the church where the Fishers attended. A strong, functional family was the usual theme.

The Catholic Church produced *Insight* which ran for nearly twenty-five years. Lesser productions by other Christian churches include *This is the Answer* by the Southern Baptists and *The Pastor* by the Methodist church.

This Day Give Us Bread

Some things are much bigger than they first seem.

The Lord's Prayer is certainly the most memorable and oft-prayed prayer in the world. Even those who do not pray recognize the "Our Father" prayer. They may even know all of the words of the prayer, given by Jesus as He sat on a mountain, teaching His disciples and the crowds that came to learn from Him. (The Sermon on the Mount, Matthew 5-9).

The prayer is prayed to the Father in heaven (the intro). It is followed by seven petitions (the "things") we ask God. I'll be brief:

- Hallowed be thy name
- Thy kingdom come
- Thy will be done on earth
- Give us this day our daily bread
- Forgive us our trespasses
- Lead us not into temptation
- Deliver us from evil

This story is about the fourth petition, our daily bread. I will let you find the meaning of the other things we ask, maybe best explained by Martin Luther in the *Small Catechism*.

God, our Father, knows what we need before we even ask. Luther explains that daily bread is more than bacon, eggs, milk, and bread. He says that daily bread means "everything that belongs to the support and needs of the body" and then he give his short list: "food, drink, clothing, shoes, house, home, land, animals, money, goods, a devout husband or wife, devout children, devout workers, devout and faithful rulers, good government, good weather, peace, health, self-control, good reputation, good friends, faithful neighbors, and the like." If pressed, I'm sure he could have listed others. So, to Luther, daily bread was (is) more than it might seem.

Why name both house and home? I find this distinction interesting. A house is simply shelter, a building of sorts. A home is much more!

Daily bread is good friends and faithful neighbors. If you are so blessed, be thankful. Not everyone is so blessed. How many folks do not know the name of even one friend? One neighbor? Good government, devout and faithful rulers? We might question that at times, but perhaps we should consider what we have compared to what many others have. What others experience every day may be much worse than what we experience.

The conclusion to the Lord's Prayer as written by Luther is not included or recited by some. I will use the more modern translation: "For the kingdom, the power, and the glory are Yours, now and forever. Amen." What a perfect ending to the prayer!

Luther says that we should be certain that these petitions are pleasing to our Father in heaven, and are heard by Him.

One more thing. When it rains, it rains on the good and the evil. When the sun shines, it's helpful and healthy for the good and the evil. When the grocery cart leaves the store... well, you get the picture. As Luther also said, "God gives daily bread without our prayers, even to all evil people."

God wants us to realize His goodness and receive our daily bread with thanksgiving.

Thanksgiving every day? Practice! Practice! Practice!

This Is the Gate of Heaven

Pastor Drew based his sermon today on the Old Testament lesson, Genesis 28:10-17; the story of Jacob's Ladder.

Jacob was on a road trip from Beersheba to Haran, and he was on foot. The sun was about to set, so he got ready for the night. He took a stone from that place and put it under his head for a pillow. I always take my pillow with me when I can. It's soft and helps to induce sleep when I'm on the road. I imagine Jacob's stone pillow was large, maybe quite flat, and not very comfortable!

Genesis 28:12 says that Jacob dreamed. Don't know what the fellow had to eat that day or what weighed heavily on his mind, but in his dream, a ladder had been set on the earth and the top of it reached to heaven. He saw angels, ascending and descending the ladder. Must have been a wide and strong ladder. The Lord stood at the top of the ladder.

God said, "I am the Lord, the God of Abraham your father and the God of Isaac. The land on which you lie I will give to you and to your offspring. Your offspring will be like the dust of the earth, and you shall spread abroad..." (Gen. 28:13-14 ESV). Then came the real message, the punchline, the promise: "and in you and your offspring shall all the families of the earth be blessed." A mission blessing.

There was more to the blessing. "I am with you and will keep you wherever you go, and will bring you back to this land. For I will not leave you until I have done what I have promised you" (Gen. 28:15 ESV).

I think most dreams are short. Some are vivid with great detail. Some may be scary. Others might be joyous and happy. Most dreams are quickly forgotten; like a fog that covers the ground and as the sun heats the earth, they disappear. Jacob's dream was memorable.

When he awoke, he said," Surely the Lord is in this place, and I did not know it." The dream frightened him, and he uttered, "How awesome is this place! This is none other than the house of God, and this is the gate of heaven" (Gen. 28:16-17 ESV). As he recalled the scene, he likely was in no hurry to go on his way, but rather lingered there.

The next morning, he continued his trek to Haran, but not before he took the stone on which he had slept, and "set it up as a pillar and poured oil on it" (Gen. 28:18). While the city there had been called Luz, Jacob named the place Bethel.

When you dream (wish) upon a star, you are likely in Fantasyland! When you dream upon a rock, that's real, man! And the Rock is the promised Savior, Jesus. Born in Bethlehem, lived, crucified, dead, and buried, but risen three days later, victorious over sin, death, and the devil, to all who believe.

FYI:

1. Bethel is Hebrew for "House of God," so some churches use that to name their church and congregation. Bethel is frequently mentioned in the Bible with reference to many of the Old Testament patriarchs.

2. Jacob's dream occurred near the modern-day village of Beitin in the West Bank where an area of springs allow for olive, almond, fig, and plum groves.

The "That" Section

That Town Drunk	73
That's the Way I Like It	75
That's It!	78
That's Life #1	82
That's Life #2	85
That's Life #3	88
That Dog Won't Hunt #1	91
That Dog Won't Hunt #2	94
That Dog Won't Hunt #3	97
Atta Boy!	99
That's Amore	101
That Formula: Healthy, Wealthy, and Wise	103
That's What I'm Talkin' About!	105
And That (My Nephew, Wayne)	107
That Don't Impress Me Much	110
That Takes the Cake	115

That's A Great Question 118

That Old-Time Religion 120

Imagine That 123

That's A God Thing 125

Oh, That I Had A Thousand Voices. 127

That's a Fact, Jack! 131

That's All She Wrote. 133

That Dr. Jeremiah 136

That's the Way the Ball Bounces 139

That's Entertainment 142

That'll Be the Day 145

That Depends. 146

El Gato Negro. 147

That'll Teach Him! 150

That Nothing May Be Lost 152

That's the Ticket 155

That's All Folks!. 156

That Town Drunk

My pastor occasionally inserts what I'll call scriptural comedy into his sermons. I'm not sure that all of the folks "get" the joke, but I can almost "see" the humor coming. I want to laugh loudly, but being in church, I and a few others practice some restraint. The humor is meaningful to the gospel text for the sermon.

The Wedding at Cana (John 2:1-12), often referred to as the first miracle of Jesus, was the gospel lesson for the day. Even people who do not read the Bible or who seldom go to church probably know the story of Jesus changing water into wine.

At some point in my early Christian education, I learned that weddings in the early church could last for a whole week or more. Jesus, His mother, and His disciples attended the celebration at Cana. There was a problem. The bride's family ran out of wine for their many guests. Mary went to Jesus and said, "They have no more wine." After He told her "His time had not yet come," she went to the servants and told them, "Whatever He says, do it!" Mary knew her Son very well!

There were six stone water pots, apparently used for the Jewish custom of purification. These were not small pots; each could hold twenty to thirty gallons. In John 2:7, Jesus told the servants to fill the pots with water, so "they filled them to the brim." I'm guessing "to the brim" is where my pastor may have noted a possible short, witty comment; a little humor (more on this in a bit).

The story continued with Jesus telling the servants to "draw some out and take it to the master of the feast (the head honcho of the catering company or maybe even the father of the bride) (John 2:8 ESV). When tasted, the water had turned to wine. The bridegroom was called. The master of the feast told the man (and I'll paraphrase a bit), "Every man, at the beginning sets out the good wine, but this wine is select, perfect. The color, the nose, the exquisite taste. Most serve the lesser wine after the folks have drunk a lot, maybe more than they should have" (John 2:10).

The Bible does not tell us how much wine the wedding party started with, but now, one hundred and fifty gallons or more was available. This wedding celebration may have lasted for many more days. My kind of party!

So, back "to the brim" thing. My pastor took that large quantity of wine and equated it to the quantity of blessings that Jesus can and does bring into our lives (e.g., forgiveness of sins, life everlasting, etc.). A dozen or more times in that sermon, he pointed to the risen Christ on the cross (always standing to the side of the pulpit) and said, "More Jesus, please! More Jesus!"

Just at the point when new, good wine is served, He says to us, "Go ahead. Drink what you want. Be that town drunk if you must." In other words, eat up, drink up, and proclaim what blessings Jesus has given to you. Be filled with Jesus as you receive His blessings daily!

So, someone says, "Jesus encouraged people to drink until sick and throwing up?"

No, you don't get it, do you?

You can get it (the bread and the wine) every Sunday at my church!

That's the Way I Like It

    aha moment: a moment of sudden insight or discovery, realization[18]
        moment: a very brief period of time[19]
    Other ways to say that: a split second, a sec, a bit, a little while

Though the connotation differs, the aha expression is used eighty-six times in the lyrics of "That's the Way I Like It" (KC and the Sunshine Band, 2012). To add to the rather boring lyrics, the song begins and ends with "do, do, do" thirty six times. What could you expect from the album called Rumba Doo Wop?

The Backstreet Boys recorded the song with different lyrics, also not very interesting, in 1997. In that version, the "aha" was replaced by "uh huh," also eighty-six times. The duration of both recordings was more than five minutes.

So, I write books, right? Now and then, I also write songs. Here's my version of the song, changing the "aha, ahas" and "uh huh, uh huhs" to "ah hum, ah hums."

I Like To Write

"I like to write,
Ah hum, ah hum,
Morning or late night,
Ah hum, ah hum,

This, That and the Other Thing

Whether song or book,
Ah hum, ah hum
No dif to me!
Ah hum, ah hum.
Sometimes at night,
Ah hum, ah hum,
New thoughts pop up,
Ah hum, ah hum,
Some good, some not so,
Ah hum, ah hum.
I write them quick,
Ah hum, ah hum,
So I don't forget,
Ah hum, ah hum.
Now as to books,
Ah hum, ah hum,
It takes a while,
Ah hum, ah hum,
Some fact, some fiction,
Ah hum, ah hum,
My readers don't care,
Ah hum, ah hum.
I like to read,
Ah hum, ah hum,
Both male and others,
Ah hum, ah hum,
Some C.J. Box,
Ah hum, ah hum,
And Sandra Brown,
Ah hum, ah hum.
Grisham is good,
Ah hum, ah hum,
Baldacci, my fav,

Ah hum, ah hum,
Ralph Kramden oft said,
Ah hum, ah hum,
'Homina Homina,'
Alice, his *Honeymooner* wife,
Just carried on unfazed.
(And then, with the well-known fade-out)
Ah hum, ah hum, ah hum, ah hum"

FYI:

Most songs recorded today are closer to three minutes in duration, thank God!

That's It!

I have recounted this story in one or more of my earlier books. I'm sure that some of my readers are tired of hearing it, but it fits so well into the "That" section of this book.

Every American kid or student, no matter their grade in school, has heard these two words with an exclamation mark after. Every parent, grandparent, or teacher has used these two words when frustrated to the endth degree. Roughly translated, the two words mean, "I've had enough," "If that continues, you'll be sorry," or perhaps, "Just wait 'til your father gets home!" There are many others such as "Not another word out of you!" "How many times have I told you...?!" "Go to your room!"

In my vocational agriculture class at Washington High School in the late 1950s, our instructor, Mr. Hall, had had just about enough from his class of about twenty boys who were anticipating lunch rather than whatever he had planned. We were not settling down for class and we wondered just how far we could push our shenanigans.

After three admonitions and the class mostly quiet, I thought one more delay would work. I rose halfway from my chair, the metal legs scraped loudly on the tile floor, and I said, "Okay, boys, jes one mo time!"

My smirk quickly vanished as Mr. Hall took me by the shirt collar and removed me from the classroom. His office was across the hall, by the vocational shop, and that's where I spent the rest of the day. No lunch, forgotten by my teacher and every one of my Future Farmers of America friends.

I happened to be the president of our FFA, so my behavior was unbecoming of an officer. But Mr. Hall's face when he found me about 3:30 p.m. told me that I had a little leverage in the situation. I didn't have to use it. Mr. Hall drove me home that afternoon after missing the bus.

Here's another scenario. Taking a ride in the old Chevy jalopy or even later in the 1955 four-door Chevy, my brother, sister, and I sometimes "acted up." When mom or dad had had enough from the back seat, an arm would come flying back at us with the warning, "That's it!" I don't recall dad ever stopping the car to find a lithe branch on the side of the road for a whipping, but back at the house, each of us had some quiet time to consider our behaviors and likely early to bed penalties.

Now, I'm going to change the subject again and get a little political as I am wont to do. This is being written in early November 2021. The Virginia and New Jersey elections for governor one week earlier resulted in an extremely close voting, especially in New Jersey, Murphy, a Democrat, was apparently the "skin-of-his-teeth" winner. McAuliffe, the former governor in Virginia, lost to the Republican challenger, Youngkin, in a not-so-close race. Republicans saw both of these as promising for the national elections in 2022.

After just ten months in office, the Biden administration had been "acting up." Our southern border was a sieve, a record number of immigrants illegally crossing into our country. Many of them were bussed to locations across the country, unannounced to state and local officials. The Department of Justice was serious about giving a half-million dollars to illegals whose child was separated from them (under Obama rules), some never to be seen again. You're kidding me, right? No! For real!

At the end of Trump's four years, America was energy independent and relied on purchasing petroleum from those who agreed to sell it. Gas at the pump was $3 to $8 a gallon, unbelievably increased in a very short time. Pipelines had been closed in the U.S. Many jobs were lost, and there was talk about closing other pipelines. The president was listening to the socialist environmentalists.

The American military departure from Afghanistan was a Biden bow to the Taliban. Billions of dollars of military resources were abandoned, left to the enemy in Afghanistan. Not all Americans who wanted to get out of the country got out. Many American supporters there were left to suffer at the hands of the Taliban.

Had enough? Control of the U.S. House of Representatives and Senate resulted in the passage of another trillion-plus dollar infrastructure bill, only a small part of which was infrastructure as we knew it. Then, before a possible Republican win in the House, Senate, or both in 2022, other trillions of dollars were being pushed for the Build Back Better Biden debacle.

Inflation was on the minds of most American people and families with little or no extra cash who struggled daily.

The supply chain of products waiting to be purchased by American consumers had not been resolved by the end of the year.

Mask mandates by the Biden blunders were about as popular as flies on the picnic potato salad.

Forced vaccinations of workers in all parts of the American economy were being popularly protested in many large cities. Racial tensions? Racial injustice? Please, don't get me started. A loud exclamation of "That's it!" was the order of the day. "That's enough! Stop it, already!"

That's It!

Someone has got to have some common sense control of our government!

Okay, so I get on my high horse politically at times, but tell me where I'm wrong.

That's Life #1

Long ago, a dozen years before my lifetime, Herbert Prior Vallee sang a song, "Life Is Just A Bowl of Cherries." Written by Lew Brown and Ray Henderson, Rudy Vallee recorded it with his band, The Connecticut Yankees.

Rudy Vallee was active in American culture for six decades, having started as a drummer in high school, and later playing the clarinet and saxophone. The attractive singer, musician, actor, and radio host was one of the first modern American pop stars with teen idols and adults who adored him.

My take on the lyrics might be different than your interpretation. A bowl of cherries? I guess that depends largely on what kind of cherries. The cherries I picked as a kid across the road from Lohmeyer's General Store in Lyon, Missouri needed a lot of sugar to make a tasty pie, jelly, or cobbler. And an undetected cherry pit could crack a tooth and cause some real pain. Life isn't always such a bowl!

The song writers say, "Don't take it (life) serious. Life's too mysterious."[20] Somehow, I don't get the sense of careless living. Carefree is maybe more to the point?

"You work, you save, you worry so," they go on, "but you can't take it with you, when you go, go, go." The fact that the song was written during our American depression years is evident, at least to me.

That's Life #1

"The sweet things in life to you were just loaned, so how can you lose what you never owned?" The song suggests that we "live and laugh at it all."

Many in my generation will remember a Frank Sinatra version of "That's Life."[21] Written by Dean Kay and Kelly Gordon, it was first recorded by Marion Montgomery in 1963. Sinatra's recording solidified the uplifting message of the lyrics.

"That's life. That's what all the people say. You're riding high in April, shot down in May. But I know I'm gonna change that tune, when I'm back on top, on top in June."

So, life's a roller coaster. It has been and can be for many. "But I don't let it get me down; cause this fine world, it keeps spinning around."

"A puppet, a pauper, a pirate, a poet, or pawn, and a king." Perhaps not everyone's experience, but for some, that's life. "I've been up and down, over and out, and I know one thing. Each time I find myself flat on my face, I pick myself up and get back in the race."

Resilience is certainly strong in the song, just as it is in our American lives. When disasters hit, whether fire, flood, tornadoes, or other storms, news reports nearly always include "We'll recover. We'll get through this. We'll be back!" American history records our recovery.

I will spare you the less positive aspect of the last two verses, but remind you of the lyrics from another song, "It's A Hard Knock Life" (Annie). Yes, trials and tribulations are part of life. That persuades me to finish with a religious note. How do people live with their hard knocks without a faith life?

No one likes to think of the end of life. It can be frightening, overwhelming, and, at least, uncomfortable, but life does go on even without us.

For Christians, the hope and real expectation of the resurrection, life is a venture in faith. It does go on! And on! And on!

Happy Easter!

That's Life #2

My family and friends know that I am big on baseball. From spring training in March through the summer All Star game and into the postseason (October), that's my life, morning, noon, and night. I purchase the added Baseball Network and can (and often do) watch three or more games a day. It's my favorite game to play (though that slowed significantly over the last ten years) and my favorite sport to follow. Those who can't stand to watch two-and-a-half hours or more of a game just don't appreciate the athleticism and the nuances of professional baseball. I live in LSU country, so the Tigers in Baton Rouge are often in the nation's top ten teams. I, however, will always be a St. Louis Cardinals fan.

One night, our pitcher worked for six or more innings on the mound, and then two or more relief pitchers towed the pitching rubber, and, often, won. Sometimes we shutout the opposition. Sometimes we lost and lost badly. We may have a measly four hits one night, then the next game gets a dozen or more base hits. The announcer for the game simply says, "That's baseball!"

The MLB schedule now includes 162 games. One season we might win ninety-plus games. The next season we may struggle to win even eighty. Again, that's baseball!

There are thirty-two major league teams. The lesser teams might only win sixty times, but the loyal fans still come back for Opening Day, pay a lot of money for a good seat, and blow $200 or more on food and drinks for a family of four. That's baseball!

This story is not about baseball, though. It's a story about life. Maybe the two are not so dissimilar?

"This Is It" is a song of the late 1970s, nearly four minutes long. Recorded by Kenny Loggins, it was the lead single in his album *Keep the Fire*. The song reached the Top 20 on the Billboard Hot 100 and #17 on the Adult Contemporary chart. Written by Loggins and Michael McDonald initially as a love song, they decided that it was boring. I'm not sure that the two revisions made it less boring or more meaningful, so my comments that follow are strictly my own.

Michael Jackson and Scotty McCreery recorded the song, each with different lyrics of sorts, and The Strokes band released it with the title "Is This It?" You can find all of the lyrics online if interested. If I counted correctly, the title is sung eighteen times as part of the chorus.

A certain fatalism pervades the Loggins version, yet he sings, "Still, sometimes I believed we'd always survive." "It's over, only if you want it to be" is sung in the pre-chorus, but the suggestion is made that, "if waiting for a sign, it may never come."[22]

Parts of the boy-girl love song are still apparent: "Let him believe, Leave him behind" and then "Know whatever you do, I'm here by your side." In the bridge, "Comes a day in every life" and then, "You make the choice of how it goes, no one can tell what the future knows."

I'll guess a little at the song's meaning:

1. We each have many questions about our world and how we live each day. We must live with the choices we make or try to.

2. The future is a puzzle, and hopefully, we find where most of the pieces fit and are content with them. We accept some frustration.

3. At times, the choices in life are imminent; there's no time for lengthy study. The choices may consume us, but just do it! This is it!

Anything new, positive, or exciting in your life?

That's Life #3

My wife and I visited New Braunfels, Texas, the San Antonio area, part of the Hill Country of the state many times when we lived in the Rio Grande Valley. We stayed at a beautiful campground called The Other Place. I called it a campground, but all of the rentals were furnished with the best. The spring-fed Comal River provided the water fun with entry spots for various float trips just yards away from each residence.

We were on my daughter's dime. Kristen made the reservations months prior just after getting her new job in Lafayette in the labor and delivery wing of the hospital. There were just seven of us, but the Zubik House had three full bedrooms, each with shower and bathroom, a small vanity in each, wonderful beds, etc. The knotty pine interior included a full kitchen with everything one would need. A large kitchen table and a second table for board games, cards, or whatever was tucked into a corner.

White-tail deer appeared in the mornings and the evenings, a half-dozen or more at a time. There were big bucks, many does and fawns. Geese, squirrels, raccoons, and several hawks were also animal attractions throughout our stay.

The middle ground inside the circular drive had seesaws, swings, and climbing structures for children and volleyball and horseshoes for the adults. Large and small smokers and grills dotted the grassy grounds, enough for every renter and barbeque enthusiast.

That's Life #3

As my son-in-law and I unloaded my truck on Thursday afternoon, a young lady walked by, tears in her eyes, bringing items from her car for a family gathering fifty yards from our house.

"How are you today?" we asked, wanting to know if she was all right.

"Not so well," she replied. "My younger brother passed away three days ago."

Our "sorry for your loss" reply was far short of what we felt at the moment. Her name was Judith.

My main job for the weekend was the grillin' job for Saturday lunch. In this part of Texas, you do your large shopping at an HEB grocery. The HEB brand is comparable to any such enterprise in the country. In addition to all of the other things you need for a weekend, I made sure that we got plenty of pork steaks, sausages, and potatoes, both regular russets and sweet potatoes. Some Sweet Baby Rays, a bag of charcoal, and lighter fluid completed my portion of the cart.

Of course, we all wondered how the young man, we'll call him Ronald, died. First thoughts ran the gamut from possible suicide to drug overdose to fentanyl poisoning (so prominent in the death of young people in our country at the time) to an unfortunate accident.

On Saturday, our curiosity grew, as three or four other houses were filled by friends and family of Ronald and Judith. Mark, Nathan, and I went over to introduce ourselves to the many folks at the tables and grills where their food preparations were happening. After telling the assembled crowd how sorry we were to get the news from Judith, two or maybe three of the family, almost in unison, chimed in, "We're having a celebration of life." Small talk continued for a moment before we left that group, feeling a little better about their "celebration."

On collecting information from the office and Mrs. Woodard, only the second family whole history includes The Other Place, I inquired about the large group at the far end of the drive.

She said that the young man had been at a party. Having had too much to drink, he called an Uber and was on his way home. Another partying youth, too drunk to drive, slammed into the Uber, killing Ronald on the spot.

I'll be fourscore years old very soon, and the story of Judith and her brother causes a lot of reflection. On the trip to New Braunfels, we were a party of seven. Grandsons who had graduated from college, both LSU, one now in dentistry in Dallas and the other in data science in Baton Rouge. Their better halves in family law and hospital dietitian, each looking forward to successful futures. As I dozed off to sleep late on Saturday, I recalled my three kids, their families, and the other eight grandkids and three great-grandkids, wondering about their future lives.

Ronald's birthday, his twentieth, was celebrated on Saturday at The Other Place. It was a beautiful day, except for the reason for gathering.

Note: Except for the name of the brother and sister, this story is true. "That's Life #3" is really shallow, of course, but life can be celebrated, even in unfortunate circumstances.

That Dog Won't Hunt #1

I think of myself as a southerner. Growing up in Missouri, undergrad for four years in Nebraska, first five years after college in Michigan, and four years of school administration in New York, and I had enough of snow, sleet, ice, and slush. I headed south as soon as I could. Boca Raton, Florida, the Rio Grande Valley of Texas, and now nearly twenty-five years in New Orleans, I have no thoughts of my life ever in the Dakotas or Minnesota.

I also think of myself as a gardener. Even in New York City, I composted leaves and vegetable matter, built up a six-inch layer of some on top of an asphalt lot, and planted flowers and vegetables. I'm sure I got my gardening lifestyle from my father, who grew enough string beans, cucumbers, potatoes, radishes, carrots, and sweet corn to keep my mom busy with canning from spring through summer and into the fall.

I think of myself as country. The saying "that dog won't hunt" is southern and country slang like "madder than a wet hen," "till the cows come home," or "hold your horses."

"That dog won't hunt" is said in response to someone's suggestion, meaning something just isn't going to happen, a claim that is not viable (unfounded, inaccurate). A fifth grade classmate of mine often said in response to some claim that I made, "It ain't done it!" In other words, "No way, Jose!" or, "I believe it when I see it!" or used by natives of Missouri, "Show me!"

This, That and the Other Thing

A political interlude:

In early March 2022, Russia's invasion of Ukraine resulted in mass immigration of Ukraine women, children, and some men to flee to Poland or other western countries. Destruction in cities large and small by Putin's artillery and other attack machinery was unbelievably cruel, killing thousands in Kharkiv, Kyiv, Mariupol, Kherson, and other locales.

The leader of Ukraine, Volodymyr Zelenskyy, spirited the citizens of his country to fight and resist the Russian onslaught. They have had success, knocking out many Russian helicopters, planes, tanks, and killing Putin's advancing troops.

Sanctions levied on Russia by our country and others seemed to be "too little, too late" once the invasion began. In other words, "that dog won't hunt!" The prediction of most was that Russia would take all of Ukraine. The hope of most was that Russia would not seek to own other lands in eastern Europe. The prayer of all was that the conflict would not employ nuclear force.

Okay, back to the south. Here are a few more southern expressions that you may have heard:

- too big for his britches
- air-up your tires
- bless your little heart
- bless your little pea-pickin' heart
- doesn't amount to a hill of beans
- I reckon
- if the creek don't rise
- if I had my druthers
- heavens to Betsy
- fixin' to
- over yonder

Other notes:

1. At the end of February 2023, I'm reviewing my "That" stories and making small changes before putting the stories on computer to send to the publisher. It's been one year since the Russian invasion began and the struggle goes on.

2. Many countries have aided the Ukraine effort to retain their lands with the U.S. being the principal benefactor. Some are tired of our financial support and wish that our government would do more to secure our borders and support our people. The war in Ukraine might continue to rage long after this book is published. Pray that the Ukraine-Russia conflict does not escalate into international warfare!

That Dog Won't Hunt #2

In mid-March 2022, the national discourse switched from the Afghanistan debacle, the illegal immigration at our southern border, COVID-19 topics, and violent crime to inflation, the energy crisis, and Russia's war with Ukraine.

The cost of everything (e.g., fuel and furniture, shoes and spaghetti, coffee and candy, tomatoes and tires, bananas and beer, etc.) has risen. In some areas, regular gasoline cost doubled in one year. Diesel fuel, largely used in the trucking industry, similarly doubled. Most reporting on these matters indicated that the increase was more a burden to low and middle income families, those fortunate to buy whatever they wanted not so much affected.

A little more than a year ago our president was Donald Trump. As he left office, the U.S. was energy independent, the number one exporter of energy. There was peace in the world. Now, Joe Biden is president, and the wants and desires of his Democrat base are governed by Green Energy enthusiasts.

In his first day in office, Joe Biden launched an all-out war on fossil fuels, the petroleum and natural gas industries. The president shutdown the Keystone pipeline, putting thousands of workers out of their jobs, and causing our country to look elsewhere for petroleum such as Russia, the Middle East, Venezuela, and even Iran. Before putting a halt to Russian imports of oil just ten days ago from this writing, our country was getting large amounts of oil from Vladimir Putin, the aggressor in Ukraine.

Those concerned about climate change and the emissions caused by petroleum refining apparently "looked the other way" knowing that oil from other countries was dirtier than the oil produced by American exploration and production.

Joe Biden stubbornly refused to open exploration and production of oil and natural gas in our country. Reports were that the known oil and gas resources in the U.S. were ample enough to provide for such for two centuries. The cost of gasoline, diesel fuel, and the hundreds of other products in the petrochemical industry appeared to be remaining at the high costs or, in fact, growing higher.

I've lived in Louisiana now for more years than in any other state. I love Louisiana Senator John Kennedy, known for his common sense thinking and quick, comic wit, appearing frequently on national news and cable stations. It was Senator Kennedy who quipped, concerning the Democrats and their hope (wish) that Green Energy sources need to be pushed at this time in our country, "Wind, solar, and pixie dust" will save the country. The Biden administration suggested that Americans purchase electric cars, those costing as much as $60,000. Again, while some might be able to fit that into their family budget, most could not.

The president actually pushed Congress to make it illegal for petroleum companies to drill for oil on federal lands. Drill permits and leases anywhere in and on offshore lands had already been stymied.

Wind? Solar? Pixie dust? In other words, Senator Kennedy suggested, "That dog won't hunt!" That's not going to happen!

Okay. You've got to start somewhere, right? The truth is, we are not prepared to go electric in purchasing and driving vehicles. We may not be prepared for that in decades. Charging stations on property? Charging stations on the road for a recharge? We've all seen gas lines when petrol was rationed.

What is the wait time for a recharge? And can automobile manufacturers make a profit selling electric vehicles?

An update: Though his environmentalist friends were sorely disappointed, Joe Biden, in March of 2023, approved the Willow project (Conoco/Philips), which will allow three oil drilling sites with Alaska's National Petroleum Reserve. Six hundred million barrels of oil is projected in the next thirty years. Some say Biden's approval is because he may soon announce his candidacy for re-election. God knows he would need something to hang his hat on in such a run!

That Dog Won't Hunt #3

I saw it on sweatshirt: "Friends are the siblings God never gave us." No one was credited with the thought, but I really like it.

I was blessed with siblings. My father had three wives, the first two of which died quite young. Dad had children with each, five of them with my mom. We have all been close, though separated by many miles (Colorado, Kansas, Missouri, Louisiana), so it is largely via phone and email. God also gave each of us many family and friends in our respective locations. My current count on grandkids is eight and four great-grandkids. Thank you, Lord!

Some of my friends agree with me politically. Others have very different persuasions. The diversity of opinions and feelings is amazing, and frankly really hard to understand. How can some of my friends be so ill-advised and laughable? The topic or issue makes no difference: political personalities, COVID mask mandates, immigration, abortion, fossil fuels, and even professional sports. Uninformed is, I think, accurate, but unintelligent and dullard might be more to the point!

You see, I believe there are two genders; the two created by God in the beginning. Yep! Male and female, each wonderfully made and specially gifted. All of the other genders in fashionable conversation today were invented (not created) by my liberal friends. Some of my Republican and/or Conservative family and friends might agree, in part, with the Democrat and woke contingent.

The transgender thing in recent years has been highlighted by a University of Pennsylvania swimmer, Leah Thomas. In the spring of 2022, Ms. Leah Thomas won the Division 1 NCAA tournament title in swimming. Her (His) time was 4:24.06 in the 500 meter freestyle, finishing 1.75 seconds ahead of a University of Virginia freshman, Emma Weyant. Ms. Weyant was the silver medalist in the 400 meter at the Tokyo Olympics. Katie Ledecky, a ten-time Olympic medalist's time in the 500 freestyle was 15:37.34. The NCAA allowed Thomas to compete. She (He) would likely win other swim events.

Many in athletic competition, especially in women's swimming, loudly shout, "That dog won't hunt!" Ron DeSantis, the Florida governor, commented on the matter and said, "This is just wrong!" and declared Emma the real winner. After all, Emma was (is) a woman! The NCAA officials chose the coward's way out, announcing "Well, it's a matter of inclusion!" Really dumb!

Leah Thomas decided a couple years previous that he was a she. So, the basic question was (is): How about fair play? As a man, Leah had a longer reach, a much different muscle mass, and therefore, a decided advantage in any swimming event.

So, will we see transgendered competition in women's golf, basketball, softball, track and field, and other sports?

A rarity in sports is for a woman to participate in what most people think are men's sports. It has happened successfully, But in the cases that I know about, the woman was not transgendered as a male. Often, that scenario is as a specialized team position; a kicker on a football team, not a tackle, running back, or cornerback.

Transgendered males in a female sport is unfair to female athletes. I say "foul" and "that dog won't hunt!" That dog won't swim, either!

Atta Boy!

A playground near Kansas City, Kansas. Summer is fading and fall is already here. Grandpa sits in the bleacher, as proud and as hopeful as all of the other parents, grandparents, and team supporters of the six-year-old baseball players.

Casey comes to bat, with base hits for the season you could count on one hand. The first two pitches are called strikes, whether they crossed the strike zone or not. Grandpa wants to close his eyes for the next pitch, but doesn't. Young Casey hits the pitch with the barrel of the aluminum Easton bat, the ball rolls past the pitcher and into centerfield. Grandpa jumps to his feet and yells, "Atta boy, Casey!"

Translation: "That's my boy! A solid single!"

Casey smiles as if he now is hitting .500 or better and hopes he can be the clean-up hitter next game. He wipes his face, repositions his hat, and waits for his teammates to "pick him up" and maybe even score a run. He'll talk about the game all the way home.

"I don't care if we ever get back!" The crowd sings.

***

The team's number one goalie was sick and didn't show for the game. The coach yells Jimmy's name and tells him that he's playing in goal today. It's his first time ever as goalie. Donning the really colorful shirt and very cool gloves, the coach says, "You're a good soccer player, Jimmy. Do your best. Be tough out there, okay?"

The under ten-year-old game is uneventful for the first thirty minutes. Only one ball came even close to the goal for Jimmy. He nearly missed the punt to put the ball in play again. Fortunately, the team is pretty good. As late as the mid-point of the second half, the score is 0-0. What's new in youth soccer? Hey, what's new in soccer?

Then the trial. With less than five minutes to play, the Cayotes' biggest striker has the ball and dribbles toward Jimmy's Bulldogs' goal. Luckily, Jimmy saw him advancing. The coach yells, "Tackle the ball, Jimmy! Knock it up field!"

But Jimmy has a better idea. As the ball enters the penalty box area, he grabs the red, white, and blue #3 ball just as Charlie Cayote gets set to hammer the ball to the net. Jimmy holds tight, preparing for the collision and maybe even a soccer cleat into his ribs. The crowd's applause brings a smile to Jimmy's coach, Ron. He yells, "Atta boy, Jimmy!"

The game ends in a tie. There's no penalty kick provision in this age group to decide a tie game. The team gathers in front of the loud applause and cheers. The high-fives between all of the players and coaches makes everyone a winner. There are a few more "Atta boys" and Jimmy asks Coach Ron if he can play goalie in the next game. "That depends on how Dennis is feeling. But, maybe, yes."

Jimmy slept in his soccer jersey on Saturday, Sunday, and Monday night. The Bulldogs now had two goalies, both trusted defenders.

That's Amore

It's funny. Interesting. Even a little strange, how one thing leads to another.

I have a friend, an elderly Filipino lady who lived across the street from me for years, and now lives just around the corner on Colombo Street. She lives by herself, though her son often drives her around as needed. Her name is Amor.

Amor called me late one night as I watched St. Louis beat Miami 9-0. She needed help fixing a backyard fence and thought I could help. I told her that I was not a fixer. I had seen Amor at St. Martin for a church garage sale a week earlier.

As I slept, relishing another Adam Wainwright win, Amor came to my subconscious thoughts. And then, as fast as a Jordan Hicks fastball, Dean Martin interrupted the dream.

Dean Martin? Yes! And oldies like me might think of Jerry Lewis, his entertainer partner for many years until their acrimonious parting in 1956. You might think of the Rat Pack (Dean Martin, Frank Sinatra, and Sammy Davis Jr.) in their Las Vegas notoriety. Then certain songs came to mind.

"Ain't That A Kick In the Head?" "Memories Are Made of This." "Volare." Upon waking, the song on my mind was "That's Amore."

What's amore? Check out the full lyrics sometime. They are very Italian, like the parents of Dean Martin.

It was a no-brainer for me to include this title in my "That" portion of the book.

FYI:

1. Jordan Hicks is one of many phenoms in MLB whose fastball pitches are delivered at 100 mph or more. He has pitched one close to 104 mph.

2. "That's Amore" was released by Capitol Studios, Hollywood in 1953; Harry Warren, composer, and Jack Brooks, linguist.

That Formula: Healthy, Wealthy, and Wise

Remember how the old saying starts? "Early to bed, early to rise," and then the kicker, "makes a man healthy, wealthy, and wise."

I've always been an early bird. I guess it was the farm life in my early years; however, the early to bed part has been a problem for me. When I don't feel well or have a cold or other illness, I may hit the bed by 10:00 p.m., but that is unusual for me. I only take a baby aspirin, supposedly to assist with blood flow. I'm fortunate that way!

I had a Johnson & Johnson booster vaccination at the airport yesterday, whether I needed it or not. The nurse said, "I see you were a Halloween baby."

I said, "Well, I usually tell people I was (am) a Reformation baby." I'm not sure if she understood that as a reference to Martin Luther and the sixteenth century church.

That birthdate is a pretty good personal evangelism entre. But I got free parking for thirty minutes in short term parking and chose not to take the opportunity to talk faith, life, and religion. The nurse also told me to sit for fifteen minutes, recommended after a vaccination. I left after eight minutes when she was not looking. That's who I am, an early bird!

Speaking of health, I am always amazed at the pharmaceutical commercials on TV. Apparently someone is slouching on the job if someone in the industry doesn't come up with a new drug or medication at least daily. The "enjoyable" part of the new drug commercials is when they tell you all the possible side effects and warnings, many of them not spoken, but in small print. Lately, I've noticed that a caveat is added, "These are not all of the possible side effects."

So, here goes: stomach pain, indigestion, nausea, flu-like symptoms, sores, rashes, vomiting, bumps on your neck, extremely low or high blood pressure, tiredness, loss of appetite, fever, muscle pain, diarrhea, hair loss, headache, backache, antisocial behavior, or thoughts of suicide. Then there's the risk of stroke, increased risk of death, uncontrollable muscle movements, leg cramps, increased heartbeat, problems with urination, chest pains, shortness of breath, oily stool, and more. Man, I need some of each of those over-the-counter and/or prescription drugs. Just tell me where I can get them! Sounds great!

The truth is, you can get them at any Walgreens, Walmart, CVS, Rite Aid, many grocery stores, a local pharmacy, etc. If your doctor won't or can't prescribe them for you, you can probably find another doctor who will.

Talking with your doctor (PC) is an important aspect of general health. Be sure to write down the questions you want to ask him or her before you go. Here's another kicker: "Tell your doctor if you've been to a place where fungal infections are common." I say to myself, "Hey, let's go to one of those places next summer with grandma and the kids for a week or two. Sounds like great fun!"

One more kicker: "Don't use if allergic." Thanks for that. I hate it when my face puffs up like a *Planet of the Apes* character when I eat peanuts with a soda or cold beer.

That's What I'm Talkin' About!

You've heard it, I'm sure. Maybe heard it more than you wanted. And though you know the intended meaning, you likely would not use it in conversation with your friends or neighbors. It has a kind of southern cousin or country boy connotation, something Clark Griswold's Cousin Eddie would exclaim. Maybe redneck? Even a racist "cracker" usage in your best Chris Rock impersonation?

So, you are at a backyard barbeque with lots of different people, and the group of guys watching the charcoal heat up is talking fishing, maybe even showing cell phone pictures of the latest take of speckled trout. One guy has just returned from Table Rock in Missouri and another from Toledo Bend on the Louisiana/Texas border. A new neighbor to the party has a crappie story he is just itching to tell.

"Y'all know where Breaux Bridge is? Up near Lafayette. There's a swamp there where I catch a lot of crappie. It's Henderson Swamp by Lake Bigeaux. Me and my two boys caught us close to thirty crappie in less than two hours. That's as good eatin' as it gets! Crappie! That's what I'm talkin' about!"

Some of the guys just focus on the charcoal and the grill. A few wander off to the beer barrel. No one asks what the daily limit on crappie happens to be or how large the fish has to be for a keeper. Other tall fishing stories follow.

This, That and the Other Thing

You are a St. Louis Cardinal baseball fan and home alone for a night game in Milwaukee. The Brewers' TV sportscasters have been unkind to your team. They even snicker a little when the Cardinals start to warm up relief pitcher Packy Naughton. You want to tell those poor sports that Packy's little brother couldn't say Parker, so Parker became Packy to the Naughton family.

The Brewers are the chief competition for St. Louis right now. It's the eighth inning and the Brewers have had a two-run lead for more than two hours. The Red Birds have the bases loaded and first baseman Paul Goldschmidt is at the plate. After taking two called strikes and with two outs, the Milwaukee relief pitcher throws one more change up and Goldschmidt cracks a long home run into the left field seats. You jump from your sofa and yell as loudly as you can since no one else in the house, "That's what I'm talkin' about!"

Yeah, you might be a redneck!

And That (My Nephew, Wayne)

I have a nephew, who is a little younger than me named Wayne. His mother, Stella, was one of my father's many children. Wayne and I grew up in the little "wide spot in the road" called Lyon, Missouri. At the time, the population of Lyon was less than twenty-five. There has been some growth in the area, the population today about fifty. On my last visit, the "city" limits had not changed. Since the 1940s, Lyon has been about the length of three football fields, Highway 185 running through it, a little west of St. Louis.

Wayne and his wife, Carole, returned to Lyon after many years away, but they always seem to be on the road (California, Colorado, the Northeast) when I visit my brother in Washington, Missouri. I sometimes stay with them if they happen to be home. The three of us like to talk. We have so much history in Missouri and both of us have families throughout our country.

When together, the conversation is mostly about our children, recent travel or adventure, the Lyon Store (which Wayne's dad owned and operated, now with new owners and offering meat processing, groceries, etc.), a little politics, religion and faith life, baseball, the weather, and other topics also come to fore when I am with the Lohmeyers.

Wayne has an unusual expression in conversation, used a lot when he chimes in. His expression of, "and that" is a little like etcetera, but different! It's one of the first things I thought of for the "That" section of this book. Here's an example or two:

Wayne: "Once when Carole and I had talked about 'God things' and that, I was walking in what had been a peach orchard when mom and dad still lived here at the house, and that. When you are off by yourself, and that, thinking about many things, and that, I don't know; you feel closer to God and what He is saying to you, and that."

Or: "We were in Connecticut with Suzanne for about five weeks, and that. Carole's mom was just out of surgery, and that, so we helped as much as we could. We'd take the kids to school, to sports, to lunch on weekends, and that."

I don't think I have gone overboard in these two examples, but as I recall several of Wayne's anecdotes, and that. The expression might be used a dozen times or more.

I have a pretty good memory. This third example might be Wayne verbatim:

"When in Connecticut, Carole often made the meals, and that. I did some small repairs on the property, and that. It was much easier for us to visit up there than for them to travel to see us in Missouri, and that,"

If and when Wayne and Carole read this, Wayne may not even be aware of his frequent use of the "and that" expression. I wonder if Carole or anyone else has called it to his attention? It doesn't really bother me and hasn't affected our visits at all. It's just unique to Wayne, and that.

Wayne was in the USAF for seven years. I envied him for that, and that. Carole was a Massachusetts girl. She enjoyed their time in England, Los Angeles, and Maine. I think she enjoys life in Lyon, just like Wayne does, and that.

When did the idiosyncrasy begin? I don't think it is or was a Missouri thing. Maybe college speech class? Officers Candidate School? A Northeastern thing?

And That (My Nephew, Wayne)

Macht nichts, and that.

That Don't Impress Me Much

Shania Twain's country song, "That Don't Impress Me Much" from 1997 is about a guy or guys who think too much about themselves. I'll forgive her use of "don't" instead of "doesn't" because one syllable rather than two fits the song's meter to make it work.

Shania sins about guys who think they are special; the know-it-alls, the geniuses, those who maybe think of themselves as an Elvis Presley or a Brad Pitt. The ones who use hair gel to keep their curly locks in place, who spend hours shining their car and warn their girl to be careful getting in so as not to track in dirt, the guy who'd kiss his car "good night." Wow! Does any guy really carry a mirror in his pocket or a comb up his sleeve for minor adjustments or touch ups just to watch a few favorite game shows? One I try to catch regularly is *The Chase*. Three contestants take a two-minute trivia cash build up quiz, netting $5,000 for each correct answer.

Whatever they make is eventually put into a team bank. These amounts tend to be in the $15,000 to $40,000 range, and they have an opportunity to increase their total depending on what the Beast offers them. That could be a lower amount or a higher amount. Each of the three must face the east (Mark Labbett) in another trivia contest to put that money in the team bank. Some are not caught by the Beast in the chase. Some are caught. So, the final chase against the Beast is sometimes all three contestants, just two of them, or even just one. If they win the chase, contestants share an equal amount of the money in the bank. If they get caught, the chase is over and the money is lost, usually the latter.

Mark Labbett is a British TV personality weighing 370 pounds. When contestants first face him, he often has a not-so-nice comment, challenging them. For example, on one occasion, after the contestant only answered three questions in the one minute time allowed, he said, "Like Shania Twain in the song, that don't impress me much."

The show host is Brooke Burns, an attractive lady who also hosts *Master Minds*, Ken Jennings being one of three trivia experts who try to outwit contestants on that show. Burns is also an actress and model.

I'm sure my readers, with the exception of my brother, Gipper, would enjoy a few trivia questions asked on *The Chase*, so, here goes:

1. What does the letter M stand for in the TV show, "MASH?"

2. Which of these explorers was born first: Christopher Columbus, Marco Polo, or Ferdinand Magellan?

3. If you are diagnosed with hypoglycemia, what do you have: high blood sugar, low blood sugar, or high blood pressure?

4. Which razor company created the first disposable razor blade? Gillette, Schick, or Williamson?

5. Before Clint Eastwood played Dirty Harry in the 1970 film, which of these had been offered the role: Frank Sinatra, Charles Bronson, or James Coburn?

6. If you are playing with a shake hand or penhold cup, what sport are you playing?

7. What kind of outdoor furniture gets its name from the mountains of New York?

8. If your food is ordered "al forno," how is it prepared?

9. What is measured on the Saffir-Simpson scale?

10. Mr. Wilson is a character in which comic strip or TV show?

9-10 correct = as good as the Beast
6-8 correct = as good as Richie (RAMA)
3-5 correct = not as good as Richie (RAMA)
1-2 correct = about as good as Gipper

Need a tie-breaker question? Which state produces about 60 percent of the eggplant in the U.S.?

And, for the geography experts: What is the most common nickname for these U.S. states?

1. MO
2. FL
3. GA
4. NY
5. NC
6. TN
7. TX
8. OK
9. CO
10. NJ

And for the "just can't get enough" trivia crowd:

1. What is the human breast bone called?
2. What is the race track where the Kentucky Derby is run each year?
3. Which European country has 26 cantons?
4. Who was the first pope (an apostle)?
5. At Oktoberfest in Germany, what is the name for the traditional men's fashion wear?

The "still not done" trivia players:

Some states in our country have two, three, or even four nicknames. One is given. Name the others:

AL (The Cotton State)

_____

DE (The Diamond State)

_____

KS (The Jay Hawk State)

_____

LA (The Creole State)

_____

MN (The Gopher State)

_____

Kinda sneaky the way I got trivia into this book, right? Let the questions that puzzled you put you to sleep tonight!

That Takes the Cake

Before I researched the expression, I wondered whether it might just be colloquial, or maybe a central Missouri thing. Perhaps it's even more specific, something only my family used. The research will come a little later.

How about an example, using the expression from a real dairy farm in New Haven, Missouri? Aunt Doris had fixed her usual, fantastic evening meal, and my mom, brother, sister, and I were hungry for just such a spread. Looking into the kitchen as we greeted the Scheer family, we could see that dinner would include mashed potatoes, sweet corn, cooked carrots, broccoli, roast beef and gravy, garden peas, and homemade bread with various jellies and jams. Much of the food had been grown in the front gardens. Dessert would be cherry pie with ice cream. Doris always had coffee, tea, and soft drinks.

Well fed, we adjourned to the living room for some conversation. The weather was cold and a bit windy. The farm work was done for the day, so we decided to leave the pinochle game for our next get-together.

As everyone settled in, Mary and Karen, Doris's daughters, shared a couple of knock-knock jokes, the really silly kind, most of which everyone had heard before. Eugene and Julius were part of the fun, and they chimed in with a few they had heard from the neighbors. My sister and I were home from school in Nebraska, so Junior asked if there were any cornfield jokes from the Cornhusker State. I volunteered one I had heard on the radio recently.

A Nebraska high school lad had made the finals of the local spelling bee. He walked to the microphone, waiting to hear his practice round word. The word was farm.

Skip had witnessed a few spelling bees and knew all the delaying tactics. He asked for a definition of the word. The teacher said, "Farm is a plot of land use for growing crops and raising livestock." Having the stage and enjoying the attention, he went through several other probing clues to the word. "Are there any alternate pronunciations? The word origin? Etc.

At this point, the frustrated teacher repeated that this was a practice round and said, "Skip, spell farm."

But Skip had one more request: "Could you use the word in a sentence?"

The teacher reluctantly replied, "Old McDonald had a farm."

"Oh!" Skip confidently said. "I think I've got it. Farm: e-i-e-i-o." Everyone at the bee loudly laughed.

Aunt Doris started picking up cups, saucers, and napkins. Still chuckling, she said, "Richard, that's a good one. That takes the cake!"

Country folks are familiar with cake walks. The "takes the cake" expression may have started with cake walks, seen at many church picnics, family reunions, and community fundraising events.

In a cake walk, donated cakes or many varieties are placed on tables and chairs are positioned in a circle around them. One cake at a time is selected, the folks buy their cake walk tickets, and find a chair. When all or most of the chairs are taken, music is played and the folks walk around in the circle until the music stops. They sit. If their chair number is called, they win the cake.

There are variations of the cake walk, of course. The winning number could be allowed to pick a cake from the many displayed. Those who did not win might be given a small prize like a cookie or a cupcake. Much information about cake walks is available on the internet. Get-togethers on Southern plantations, both before and after Emancipation, began in the mid-nineteenth century, and that may be part of the cake walk history.

The expression can be said either positively or negatively. Positive? The Aunt Doris example. Negative? "Wow, Larry, that's the last time we'll let you pick the lunch spot!"

I thought a few corny farm jokes might be in order:

1. Where dos a farmer get his medicine?
Answer: At his farm-assist

2. What did the baby corn say to the mama corn?
Answer: Where's popcorn?

3. How did the organic vegetable die?
Answer: Natural causes

4. What do you get when you cross a robot with a tractor?
Answer: A trans farmer

5. What do you get when you cross a chicken with a cement mixer?
Answer: A brick layer

6. How does a chicken feel after laying an egg?
Answer: Egg-hausted

That's A Great Question

When you watch a news broadcast, whether local or national, and a reporter or commentator interviews someone, an interesting interaction often takes place. A question is posed. The response is often, "That's a great question!" What is really happening there?

I think it is rare if the reply is meant as a compliment, though it sounds like that. More often than not, I think it's a stall tactic. If a politician is asked the question, it's his/her way of taking a second or two to gather thoughts and then offer a relevant comment. Politicians all seem to have the gift of gab. When the interviewer wants a "Yes" or a "No" reply, that almost never happens, either.

Some skirt the issue and go off on another track, causing a repeated question or maybe a restated query. The second effort by the respondent is often no more enlightening or helpful.

Listeners are wont to say, "What? Just answer the question!" Political debates are prime examples of this.

What (Who) does "word salad" bring to your mind? Maybe Vice President Kamala Harris? Perhaps she has not had enough political experience to field questions, especially if they are of the "hardball" variety? She was the first of many Democrat candidates to bow out of the 2020 Democrat primary campaigns, and as VP, her performance has been almost embarrassing. If she follows with or combines her "word salad" with a characteristic cackle, she, again, demonstrates a lack of professional, prepared prowess.

Of course, her handlers are well aware of her poor or insufficient preparation to field questions. So, on the rare occasions when Vice President Harris is out on her own and is asked six questions, you might hear the initial, "That's a great question," response for each one. That could get real tiresome, but she needs all the time she can get to come up with something that actually makes sense. I think her usual laughter also betrays any thoughtful, professional answer.

That Old-Time Religion

What are the several items you'll see as you choose a pew in a Christian church, besides the usual "up front" things? A hymnal or song book? A Bible? Perhaps a visitor's card or an offering envelope?

There are two hundred Christian denominations in our country. How many different hymnals do you suppose are currently in use in those churches?

The research is a bit sketchy on hymnals, and the stat I found surprised me. Three hundred and twenty-one different hymnals are being used. I thought the number of denominations and the number of hymnals would be far fewer.

Four different hymnals are currently in use in my church: the Lutheran Church-Missouri Synod. Three have been published since 1978. The old one that I sang from as a kid was published in 1941.

The southern gospel hymn, "Give Me That Old Time Religion" (oft found as "Gimme That Old Time Religion") dates from 1873. The hymn is said to be a standard in many Protestant hymnals, but it is not included in any of the four LC-MS books.

The lyrics for the hymns vary from hymnal to hymnal. The first line of each verse is repeated two more times, and then a fourth or fifth line follows:

That Old-Time Religion

"Give me that old time religion.
Give me that old time religion.
Give me that old time religion.
It was good for our mothers.
It's good enough for me."

The fourth line in other verses include:

"It makes me love everybody."
"It was good for the Hebrew children."

The original hymn was written by Charlie Haden and Hank Jones. Many country and western artists recorded the song such as Dolly Parton, Johnny Cash, Marty Robbins, the Oak Ridge Boys, Buck Owens, Ernie Ford, Chrystal Gayle, and Jim Reeves. The Gospel of Jesus Christ is not mentioned in any of the hymn versions.

If there is an old-time religion, that presupposes that there is a new-time religion. Conservative pastors and national leaders of Christian churches will tell you that the "new" are too much about me and too much about you, leaving Jesus's preaching and teaching and His crucifixion out of the thinking.

If "Gimme That Old Time Religion" included the grace of God in some way and the sacrificial death of Christ for our redemption, it still might not rank up there with "Amazing Grace" or "How Great Thou Art" or "Know That My Redeemer Lives." Certainly it would be in the spiritual hymns with "What A Friend We Have In Jesus."

An individual who helped to bring "Give Me That Old Time Religion" into white audiences was Charles Davis Tillman. The Fisk Jubilee Singers were part of the song's early popularity and history.

FYI:

The Center for the Study of Global Christianity reports a staggering 45,000 Christian denominations globally.[23]

Imagine That

Considering the many television, movie, and technology industries in the U.S., who would you name as the most imaginative person of the last one hundred years?

Many parents, young adults, and children would likely say Walt Disney. Anyone who has visited Disneyland in California (opened July 17, 1955) or Disney World (opened October 1, 1971) would recall their adventures in the Magic Kingdom, Animal Kingdom, or EPCOT, and the exciting rides, food stops, stores, and parades in the amusement parks.

Younger children, including toddlers, enjoy just seeing all of the Disney wonders such as the Disney characters walking the wide and extra clean streets with them (Mickey and Minnie Mouse, Alice, Cinderella, Winnie the Pooh, Goofy, Simba, Tinker Bell, Eeyore, and others). The photographs and videos taken at the park are brought home to be seen many times over.

Who hasn't enjoyed the relaxing float trip and song of "It's A Small World" especially after a lengthy wait in line on a hot Florida or California day. Somehow, that song has a lasting quality, never to be forgotten.

The kid-friendly rides like Buzz Lightyear's Space Ranger Spin, Dumbo the Flying Elephant, the Spinning Teacups, Peter Pan's Flight, and Ariel's Undersea Adventure, and the more adventurous attractions like Space Mountain, Big Thunder Mountain, Tower of Terror, the Matterhorn, Fast

Track, Soarin', and Indiana Jones give one plenty to dream about and imagine again once the head hits the pillow at the many hotels at the parks.

Walt Disney's initial attempts at fun and folly had limited success as well as some downright failures. When he partnered with his brother, Roy, and produced "Alice in Cartoonland," successes followed. Mickey Mouse debuted in "Steamboat Willie," the world's first synchronized sound cartoon (November 1978).

Lodging for park guests added greatly to the Disney attendance at both locations. The Art of Animation, Caribbean Beach, Polynesian Village, Fort Wilderness, and Pop Century are all popular lodging choices.

Space exploration got its serious start just seventy years ago. In 2022, a small number of earthlings have taken rocketry into outer space and returned to Earth. What will the exploration story be in 2400?

What are the other areas where imagination can run wild? Medicine? Agriculture? Automation? Energy? Travel?

I recall many Saturday nights with Disney shows on the black and white TV. They always began with the signature imagination song, "When You Wish Upon A Star." Dreams can come true, at least, on the days and nights at Disney.

That's A God Thing

This is an expression that I've heard a lot recently. I hear it from people who may have dropped out of church and regular worship life, but, who now, come back to realize God in their life, at least somewhat. They may have experienced a miracle of sorts in their family or among their friends. Maybe they were surprised by a personal success? A business blessing? A general blessing in their community? They tell you, "It's a God thing, you know?"

I don't particularly like the expression, but I don't doubt the sincerity, either. I'm not doubting that such things happen in life. It just seems to make a little "light" of what I've always known: God is good!

Now, I'm going to be a little "light" in theology, a little less traditional or old school. Here's a verse from the hymn "God Is So Good" that can be sung with little children, with young people, and with your older family and friends. You could even include it as a song in church!

The song has very simple lyrics, the title repeated three times at the start:

"God is so good!
God is so good!
God is so good!
He's so good to me!"

You can make up your own verses of thanksgiving such as "He gives us life" (repeat three times). Finish with "He's so good to me."

Here's some suggested first lines, to be repeated:

"He loves me so!"
"He teaches me!"
"He cares for me!"
"He forgives me!"
"He died for me!"
"He rose for me!"
"I love Him so!"
"I praise Him now!"

Feel free to make up your own verse(s), but always finish with, "He's so good to me!"

That's our God thing! Though a bit trite and really simple, goodness is one of the many attributes of God: infinite or eternal, immutable (unchanging), omniscient, omnipresent, omnipotent, faithful, just, merciful, gracious, holy, and glorious.

Oh, my God! (which, with a little tweak, could also work as a verse).

Oh, That I Had A Thousand Voices

A Christian hymn, right? Probably sung one or more times each year if you went to church regularly.

Think back to your grammar or language classes in seventh and eighth grade. How would you Conjugate the title of the hymn? Even if you would treat those words as a beginning clause and continue with the hymn to complete the sentence or thought ("to praise my God with a thousand tongues"), there are parts (words) that would be hard to place in the conjugation (words like "oh," "that," and "I").

It's been nearly seventy years for me, and I'm not sure if junior high or middle school students are still taught conjugation in English class. I asked a few adults my age if they did conjugation of sentences in elementary school. I got mostly blank stares.

The definition I found on my phone may not help much, either. Conjugation is "the variation of the form of a verb in an inflected language by which are identified the voice, mood, tense, number, and person." [24]Huh?

Tense? Okay, I got that. But voice, mood, number, and person? An inflected language? As I remember conjugation, the teacher would write a sentence on the chalkboard (yes, what was used long before white boards and individual computers), then ask one or more students to come to the board and conjugate the sentence. If done correctly, you'd have a long, horizontal line, the subject and verb of the sentence separated by a vertical line, and numerous other lines of various slants extending from that line to indicate adjectives, adverbs, objects (either direct or indirect), prepositions, etc. Each of those was a modification noted in the subject and predicate.

The final, skeletal product on the board, especially for a lengthy sentence, looked like runways at the Atlanta Hartsfield Airport.

You recall this now, or is conjugation still a blur for you? A lost, grammatical art?

Some in my acquaintance say I'm a little wordy. Others say I'm a lot wordy. So, sorry about the verbose tangent. Now, back to the hymn.

The hymn writer of "Oh, That I Had A Thousand Voices" Johann Mentzer (1704) expressed the wish of having many voices with which to praise God. "What great things God has done for me, soul and body strangely joined, kind Guardian, all the noble joys I find, God's compassion that ransomed me. He made me His own, He gave me peace, He gave me a place among the saints, all things by His grace alone." [25]

Having a thousand tongues to express thanksgiving, you may think you might run out of things to thank God for, but no, definitely not! Not when considering the daily blessings and more mundane things of life. When was the last time we (you) sang praises to God for:

- the sun, which rises each morning without fail?

- the blue sky, while not seen every day, is still out there?

- water for drinking, washing, cooking, freezing, irrigating, swimming, or just splashing into at a beach?

- transportation to get you from here to there at the start of an ignition?

- oil and gas, pumped and processed from the earth in seemingly endless supply?

- electricity which, at the flick of a switch or press of a button, allows light in a dark house, entertainment in SO many venues, heat in the cold and cold in the heat?

- a stocked pantry, or several, with supplies for months or more?

- a half-dozen shoes to wear on your feet (or a hundred shoes, in extreme cases)?

- clothing for every kind of weather?

- a bed to sleep in?

- a gazillion plants, shrubs, trees, and grasses to enjoy right outside the front door?

- farms and farmers who continue to amaze?

- fish and other wildlife to entertain and feed us?

- the birds and bees and all that that entails?

- a toilet that flushes and plumbing people who can fix things if the toilet doesn't flush? (Research sometime to find out just how many of Earth's nine billion people DO NOT have indoor plumbing!)

- the medical field who never run out of questions and answers?

- law enforcement and safety personnel who protect us day and night, always with the threat of their own safety?

- family and friends, neighbors? (Some have none; not even one.)

The list could go on and on. Maybe you have not considered some of the above. The list of blessings that you make could far exceed mine. Put yourself to sleep tonight starting a list of your own.

Oh, that we had two thousand voices to praise our God with two thousand tongues! Oh, and where do you put that "Oh" when conjugating the sentence?

That's a Fact, Jack!

Does the title remind you of anyone? Especially if thinking of memorable movie lines? Though I'm not an avid movie person, I have seen a few and this line, "That's a fact, Jack!" reminds me of Bill Murray in the 1981 film *Stripes*. Murray was the lead character, along with Harold Ramis, John Candy, and others. Ramis wrote the script, along with Len Blum and Dan Goldberg.

John Winger (Murray) after a long line of losses (his job, his girlfriend, his apartment, and car), decides to join the army. In a spoof of basic training, Winger organizes a highly coordinated drill team. When watching the team perform with great precision, full uniform, guns and all, you almost want to give the irreverent guys a standing ovation. The base commander questions Winger, saying, "I understand that you trained the men yourself. Is that right?" With a bit of a smirk, Winger responds in drill sergeant cadence, "That's a fact, Jack!" The "boom shaka-laka" and other facetious team's chants in unison, army-style, brings laughter and enjoyment to some in the assembled crowd, if not to the more sober army brass.[26]

Another lead actor's line, this one from the *Dragnet* TV series (1951-1959), comes to mind. Jack Webb, Los Angeles Police Sergeant Joe Friday, questions a witness, in his signature low-key, tough guy role. "Just the facts, ma-am!"

In the political discourse of 2022, facts are hard to distinguish. Near mid-year, the Biden Administration announced a possible Bureau of Misinformation. Apparently, they decided that they had the facts and would dispel the opinions of their political counterparts if they differed from their thinking. That plan failed miserably, either for lack of support by their own party or the emerging distrust of socialist policies in America.

The transgender controversy was also a hot topic the first half of the year. Missouri Senator Josh Hawley at a Senate Judiciary Committee hearing questioned Khiara M. Bridges (U.C. Berkeley), who was invited by Democrat leaders. Professor Bridges indicated that some men, some transmen who are capable of pregnancy, and some non-binary people could get pregnant. This was not conjecture on her part. She actually believed what she said.

What are the facts, Jack? Are there two sexes, male and female, or more than two? A pregnant man? Does a man have regular ovulation, a uterus, and a womb?

It was reported that one Democrat at the hearing disagreed with Professor Bridges. It begs the question, what do President Biden, Kamala Harris, Nancy Pelosi, Chuck Schumer, and others in the party believe about men giving birth to a child? I'd like to hear Joe Friday's question to Khiara, "Just the facts, ma-am." Rather than ever using the term woman, she substituted the expression "People with the capacity for pregnancy."

These progressive Democrats are insanely ignorant. Do they make these things up and talk themselves into believing what they preach? Their candidate in Pennsylvania (the unkempt one) has ridiculous beliefs and stated policies. Ditto in Georgia. How can people vote for such unAmerican ignorance? Anyone remember Joe Biden's claim, "We choose truth over facts," at the 2020 Iowa State Fair?

That's All She Wrote

What does county music mean to you? For most folks, whether country music enthusiasts or not, a top three or even a top five is rather automatic: heartbreak, divorce, beer, bars, and booze, and maybe trucks and trains. Others think of automobiles, the blues, cowboys, and sad songs.

My first thought was a combination of heartbreak, relationships, and sad songs. How about the "Dear John" letter? In the 1953 song written by Billy Barton, Fuzzy Owen, and Lewis Talley during the Korean War conflict, a soldier gets a letter from his sweetheart and, somehow, the greeting is ominous: "Dear John." This is not going to be good! The song by that title was popularized by Ferlin Husky and Jean Shepherd.

The letter begins, "How I hate to write, but I must tell you tonight, my love for you has died." And the clincher, "Tonight I wed another." To add insult to injury, "The another is your brother, Don."

The "Dear John" letter is most often associated with the soldier in the field getting notice from back home that the relationship is over. Nothing more must be said.

The Korean War followed closely after World War II. The "Dear John" expression was first used in 1945.

I like country music, old and new. I tried to focus on the sad song concept, and the following songs came to mind:

- "Are You Lonesome Tonight?" by Elvis Presley
- "I'm So Lonesome I Could Cry" by Hank Williams
- "Sunday Morning Coming Down" by Johnny Cash
- "He Stopped Loving Her Today" by George Jones
- "Blue Eyes Crying In the Rain" by Willie Nelson
- "Live Like You Were Dying" by Tim McGraw

Then I researched sad country songs and many others were also familiar:

- "I Fall To Pieces" by Patsy Cline
- "Your Cheatin' Heart" by Hank Williams
- "Cold Cold Heart" by Hank Williams

The country expression "That's all she wrote" has the same meaning: an unforeseen end to one's hopes and dreams. So sudden! Out of the blue!

How about these? Not as sad, but still, sung with a bunch of emotion:

- "I Will Always Love You" by Dolly Parton
- "Concrete Angel" by Martina McBride
- "When I Call Your Name" by Vince Gill
- "I Drive Your Truck" by Lee Brice
- "Always On My Mind" by Elvis Presley, and later by Willie Nelson

Neil Diamond recorded "Song Sung Blue" in 1974. More contemporary than country, the mood is the same. Part of the lyrics say, about feeling blue, "Everybody knows one." At the start of the song, "Me and you are subject to the blues now and then."[27] It reminds me of my older brother, who lost his wife to cancer and other complications.

When I call him, though his daughter and son-in-law spend lots of time with him, as do I and other family, he never fails to mention to me, in answer to the question, "How you doin'?" "Well, same ole, same ole; lookin' at the four walls." And, wouldn't you know it, there's a country song about that, too: "Hello Walls" by Willie Nelson (1965).

Do you talk to yourself? Do you talk to your pets? Your plants? In the "Hello Walls" song, the lonely guy also talks to the window and the ceiling.

"Hello walls, how'd things go for you today? Don't you miss her, since she up and walked away? And I'll bet you dread to spend another lonely night with me. But lonely walls, I'll keep you company."[28]

It is said, "Misery loves company!" Next time you are feeling a little blue, find one or more sad country songs on the internet, play the video, and sing along. There's no guarantee that you'll be happy as a lark and feel better, but you might feel a little country, and feeling country is not all bad. And a little tear in your eye testifies to your true emotions; your love for others in your life.

That Dr. Jeremiah

Routine. We never consciously think of them, but we all have numerous routines. The morning "get up fifteen minutes later" routine. The personal exercise routine. The homemade chili routine (and hundreds of other recipes and in-the-kitchen tasks).

My daughter is an RN in labor and delivery. She is also a personal trainer. Her "open the gym for her first clients" routine takes less than five minutes, but involves a dozen little jobs, performed daily. A grandson dentist in Dallas has a ten minute "first patient" routine (check the x-ray, greet the first patient of the day, and a cursory look in the mouth).

Think for a moment of your various routines, whether daily or those special times in your week, month, or year.

It's Tuesday morning, about 6:00. St. Louis lost to Cincy last night, and I take no pleasure in a rehash of the game, usually done on *Quick Pitch* on the MLB Network. Here's a slightly condensed version of my "wake-up to a seat on the sofa" routine.

It's still dark in the house, so I turn on a lamp in the TV room and the small light above the stove. I put some water in the Keurig and insert a K-Cup, close the lid, push the "go" button and wait for the brew. Get a spoon, a bite of something, and the 2% from the fridge, and shake a 81 mg aspirin from the bottle. The day is like any other day in my kitchen.

That Dr. Jeremiah

I like hot coffee, so after the milk and a stir, I microwave for one minute. A granola bar or other breakfast treat is thrown on the couch during the reheat. I push the button at the top right for the TV, and though twenty years old, the TV still comes to life. I've had a new "still in the box" TV set for six months now, doubling as a clothes hanger, when I thought the small widescreen was going kaput.

A preacher is on. In this case, teaching a large group of adults with the topic, "The Ten Questions Christians Ask Most." For this session, the question is "What the greatest Commandment?" I've never seen David Jeremiah before. I'm inclined to change channels to the Weather Channel, ESPN, Fox and Friends, or even the local news in New Orleans, but there's something I like about the man. He has a great teacher presence. I decide to watch his Bible lesson, not my usual TV fare. Jeremiah's pretty good!

Dr. Jeremiah explains that there are more than ten commandments in the Bible. In fact, he says, there are more than six hundred laws in the two testaments. Who knew? But centering on the most important commandment, he uses Matthew 22:35 and following for the answer.

> "Then one of them, a lawyer, asked Him a question, testing Him, and saying: 'Teacher, which is the great commandment in the law?' Jesus said to him, 'You shall love the Lord, your God, with all your heart, with all your soul, and with all your mind. This is the first and great commandment, and the second is like it, you shall love your neighbor as yourself' (Matt. 22:35-39 NKJV).

As I listened to Dr. Jeremiah, his message sounded very much like the theology I learned as a kid in Sunday school, two Lutheran elementary schools, and four years of Lutheran college. Doing good things for others and loving others like you love yourself doesn't get you any closer to heaven (salvation), but it does demonstrate your love for God, which is of most importance.

As I left the house, went through my usual bike riding routine, I felt really good about a lot of things. Even better than a Cardinal game with Cincinnati in game number three of their series (a 13-inning win with star performances from Albert Pujols and Lars Nootbaar). St. Louis may win the NL Central after trailing Milwaukee all season. I'm pumped! I'm jacked! Can't wait for the Dodger series.

FYI:

Dr. Jeremiah is the founder of Turning Point Radio and Television Ministries. He is pastor of the Southern Baptist megachurch Shadow Mountain Community Church in El Cajon, California. His church has eight satellite locations, including one Hispanic and one Arabic congregation. Need a lift? A new outlook on life? Try Dr. David Jeremiah. He's pretty good!

That's the Way the Ball Bounces

Most balls are round (baseball, tennis ball, basketball, golf ball, volleyball, etc.). The football, however, is the weird one, at least, in the way it bounces.

Ask any of my family or friends, "What's Rich's favorite ball game?" and they'll answer, "Baseball." Some may go right to my favorite team and say, "The St. Louis Cardinals." Why are they my favorite team?

Maybe it was Uncle Virgil. He and my aunt Dottie lived in a trailer on the south-side of our house in Lyon, Missouri for a while when I was a kid. Uncle Virgil was a hunter, fisherman, and great storyteller. He had a large gash on his face, rolled his own cigarettes, and often, especially in the summer, rooted for the St. Louis Cardinals. Busch Stadium was just a one-hour drive from Lyon, though more ball games were played during the day rather than at night in the 1940s, 50s, and 60s. Uncle Virgil and I often spent time on a blanket in the shade of our front yard, listening to Harry Carey's radio broadcast of the games. When the blanket got a little damp from the nighttime dew, we'd go into the house and listen to the game.

Maybe it was Rube Depperman? Rube and Delphrine lived on the other side of the highway from our house. He was the fellow who operated the Lyon Feed Store and Mill after my dad retired. Rube was a hunter, owned several coonhounds, and was quite a storyteller himself. Rube was also a Red Bird fan. He told me check who was winning the division by July 4. Those one or two teams, if records were similar, would win the pennant that year. Rube was rarely wrong.

The following is a story I wrote in early September 2022. The Cardinals were seven or more games ahead of the Milwaukee Brewers, the two teams at the top of the NL Central all season. There were just thirty games left, then the playoffs and the World Series. St. Louis is a great baseball city. The Cardinal fans, many from the states that border Missouri, are baseball knowledgeable. They follow and respect the talents of the competitors on the diamond. Except for the New York Yankees, the Cardinals have won more World Series titles than any other teams.

This season, St. Louis had a very young and skilled team, but also a few veterans (Yadier Molina, Albert Pujols, Adam Wainwright). One of the youngsters was Lars Nootbaar (his full name being Lars Taylor-Tatsumi Nootbaar). His father is of Dutch, English, and German descent; his mother is Japanese. He is the great-grandson of Herbert Nootbaar, businessman and philanthropist, the highest level of professional baseball in the Netherlands. I tell you this history of Lars essentially to get my son-in-law, Mark, into the story.

Mark became a baseball fan because of me. Sometimes, we have phone conversations while watching Cardinal games. In a recent contest with the Cincinnati Reds, Lars Nootbaar played a pivotal role in a 13-inning game, won by the Cardinals. I was on the road and not able to catch the exciting extra inning game on TV, so Mark brought me up to speed the next morning. It took a while for Mark to know the St. Louis players like I knew them, so he explained to me, "In the thirteenth inning, that new guy, the one with the unusual name, Nutbomb, hit a game-winning homerun."

I thought I'd never stop laughing. Nutbomb?!

In St. Louis, when Lars makes a great play or just comes to bat, often as the team's leadoff batter, the fans go crazy, yelling, "Noot! Noot! Noot!" With many stars on the team, Lars Nootbaar has a great following, and is one of my half a dozen favorites. Nootbomb will always be a baseball memory with Mark and me!

That's Entertainment

Fifteen years ago, while browsing at my local Barnes & Noble Bookseller, I came across a title that piqued my interest. I guess you'd have to be a trivia person to actually take it home and read it, but it's a book that might be read in a few hours while having coffee at the store.

The Book of Useless Information by Noel Botham is an interesting read, just in case one day you challenge Ken Jennings on *Master Minds* or try to escape the chase of Mark Labbett, referred to on the show as The Beast, both TV productions on the Game Show channel.[29]

Botham apparently had help from The Useless Information Society, a group of thirty or more individuals who know and share their information of useless things. So, while I could have put this item in "The Other Thing" section of this book, I'm including it in the "That" section, using items from their chapter on "That's Entertainment"[30] and one or two other places.

Many actors have played the role of James Bond, but only two (at least, at the time) played Bond only once: David Niven and George Lazenby. Can you name one or two others who were cast as James Bond?

Charlie Chaplin once won third prize in a Charlie Chaplin look-alike contest.

One of the characters of the TV show *MASH* (Mobile Army Surgical Hospital) Jamie Farr was the only one of the cast who actually served as a soldier in the Korean War.

Felix the Cat was the most popular cartoon character, prior to the appearance of Mickey Mouse. Felix also was the first cartoon character in a balloon parade.

Is this useless stuff fun or what?!

One of the items in this book is about to change. Try this one the next time it's your turn to introduce a topic when everyone else in your group has said their piece. The first time the "f-word" was spoken in a movie was by Marianne Faithful in the 1968 film *I'll Never Forget What's'isname*. Brian de Palma's *Scarface* just sixteen years later uses the word 206 times, an average of once every twenty-nine seconds. Do you remember who Scarface was in our history?

The first real motion picture theater was called a nickelodeon. Admission was only five cents (Mckeesport, Pennsylvania, June 19, 1905). What did you pay the last time you went to the picture show?

The Academy Awards given out during World War II were not made of metal. Can you guess what they were made of then? Do you know what these awards are made of today?

Useless information, right? When will I ever need to know this stuff?

The movie *King Kong* was made in 1933. Do you know the year of the sequel, *Son of King Kong*?

Gone With the Wind (1939) was an epic movie of Civil War times. Do you know what's unique about that Clark Gable-Vivian Leigh classic, among all the other films of that era?

Not every author successfully sells his/her books, no matter how many books are written. I can attest to that fact, Jack! Herman Melville's timeless classic of the sea sold just fifty copies during his lifetime.

I guess I should first ask you to estimate the population of Iceland. Here's a bit of useless information about Iceland while you contemplate the question (or quickly ask Siri). The people of Iceland read more books per capita than any other people of the world. What is the population of that island country?

    A. 365,000
    B. 450,000
    C. 900,000

In the Navajo language, Kemosabe means "soggy shrub." Good thing the Lone Ranger was not fluent in the language of his subordinate Indian sidekick!

The inventor of the modern toilet in the late eighteenth century was T. Crapper. So, let's see. Is there some useless information that could come from that innovation?

A palindrome is a word that is the same if read from either the left or the right side (e.g., kayak, racecar).

Ten body parts are only three letters long. Can you name all ten? If not, let that puzzle put you to sleep tonight.

Hawaii has just twelve letters in their alphabet. Hawaiian words do not contain consonant clusters. Kahlua, therefore, is not a Hawaiian word. Maybe let Kahlua put you to sleep tonight.

That'll Be the Day

Are there some things about which you can be certain? Some rock solid happenings in life? Without a doubt? If you live in International Falls, Minnesota, you can be sure that your winter will be long and icy cold. In Miami, the 70 degree cooler air may not be experienced until December. You can also be rather certain that much of the winter will be warm and not cool.

Believers in Christ can be certain of salvation. By grace and through faith are you saved, and only because of Jesus. And we all know the two things in life that we can be certain of: death and taxes.

In the Buddy Holly song "That'll Be the Day," he was sure that his girlfriend would not leave him. The song was first recorded by Buddy Holly and the Tunes. Holly and Jerry Allison wrote the song. It was re-recorded by Holly and the Crickets. Other versions followed including one by The Quarry Men, later known as the Beatles.

How certain was the song writer?

"Well that'll be the day when you say goodbye. Yes, that'll be the day when you make me cry, You say you're gonna leave me, you know it's a lie, 'cause that'll be the day when I die."[31]

That Depends

I needed no internet for this one.

"Mommy, can I have ice cream for dessert?"
"That depends, baby
"Yeah, I know. When I eat all my carrots."

"Do I really need four tires?"
"Yes, sir. All four, and the spare is worse than the others."
"How about just two new for now, for the front?"
"That depends on the risk you want to take. Your trip is to Atlanta, right? Next week?"

"So, Dad, I can drive the Camry to college, right?"
"That depends on several things."
"Please, Dad! I need a car on campus."
"Save four hundred dollars by August 15, for gasoline, and the Camry will be off to school."
"Okay! Okay! Gee, dad, anything else?"
"How much time you got, Son?"

El Gato Negro

The first draft of this story was "That Cat," but in deference to my one semester of high school Spanish, I decided to go with the Spanish version. And, I think, the black cat story does fit nicely into the "That" section of this book.

More than a year ago, a black male cat began frequenting my address on Centaur Street. Usually when a neighborhood cat visits me, I attempt to discourage them. At this point in my life, I can do without a house pet. When Barbara was with me, we always had one or more feline fixtures, their territory both inside the house and outside.

I spend a lot of time outside gardening, reading, writing, and enjoying the fresh air, the temperature of the air not a factor. So, this cat l did not frighten in any way, and eventually, we became good friends.

The thing is, this cat belongs to a neighbor who lives on Telestar, around the corner to the south. I know this because those neighbors, either the man or the woman, have seen the fellow hanging out with me and they told me El Gato Negro is their cat. I was very willing to live with that understanding. The problem is, he likes my yard (house) better than their yard (house).

The Telestar folks named him Herbert or some ridiculous other name. I call him Black Jack, solid black hair with some golden dark brown hair when the sunshine strikes him just right. Black Jack has wonderful green eyes and a very small white spot under his chin. Cute!

After a few months, I started a feeding regimen with him (even though I didn't want to). I bought some Temptations treats (catnip, chicken, beef, salmon) which he liked. That developed into wet food, one or more times a day. Black Jack is very particular. He will not eat pate and likes his meat without carrots, rice, or other accouterments. I've never admitted to the Telestar folks that I feed Black Jack. I wonder if (and when and what) they feed him? He's kind of a gourmet cat, favorites being Sheba cuts in gravy and Fancy Feast tidbits, again, with gravy.

Once, my son, Joe, and his wife, Marian, and possibly a few grandkids were at my house visiting. Well, Mr. and Mrs. Telestar show up, looking for Herbert. Joey apparently heard a faint bell or signal of sorts in my carport boxes, and that happened to be an orange cat necklace with all the bells and whistles to indicate the location of the cat. There is some dispute about the brief interchanges between Joey, Marian, and the cat's legal owners. I recall it went something like this:

"Is this thing your cat's necklace?" Joe asked at the sidewalk.

"Why, yes, it is. Where did you get it?" the mister wondered.

"I heard something ringing and took it from one of my dad's boxes."

The mom inquired, "Has he been eating at this house?"

Marian offered, "Oh, yeah, grandpa feeds him all the time."

Gee, thank you, Mare. Now what?

El Gato Negro

Somehow, the episode ended and my relationship with the neighbors continued without great animosity. I chose to welcome Black Jack whenever he came over.

Mr. Telestar comes searching for the cat often, mostly in the evening and on weekends. If he finds him, he speaks gently to the cat, picks him up, and carries him back to his other house. I have no problem with that, but I do wonder if they lock him up at times or even mistreat him.

Apparently, you can buy all manner of GPS items to attach to an animal. I've never removed any of those from Black Jack's neck. I've never even picked the cat up or caressed him like you know who. Black Jack has never been in my house and that practice will continue. I love his little routine when he comes for breakfast, lunch, or dinner. He waits patiently at the door, expecting his usual. I rub his head and nose a little, and his back and tail after presenting the entree on a clean saucer or plate.

"Hey, kitty cat. Hungry? You wait here. I'll be right back. I love you, Black Jack. You are always welcome at my house."

That'll Teach Him!

A young father sits on the bathroom floor, not looking very well. He sips cautiously from a 28-ounce grape Pedialyte, eyes closed, a real case of dehydration. Maybe stayed too long at the fair? His six-year-old daughter spots him clutching her Pedialyte and says, "Hey, that's mine!"

She runs to her mom and says, "Mommy, I think daddy is kind of sick. What's wrong with him?"

"Daddy will be okay, honey; he just needs a little time to recover. He had a little too much fun at our party last night."

Katie checks on her father, gulping the Pedialyte now. He looks at his little girl and says, "I'll buy you a pony."

Returning to the kitchen, Katie says, "Daddy said he's going to buy me a pony."

"He did, did he? Well, we'll have to talk about that, okay, sweetie? Come to the store with me. We'll get you some more Pedialyte. Daddy has to stay home and clean the bathroom. That'll teach him!"

Hydration! We all need it at times. Some more than others!

FYI:

This story was written just after I saw the Pedialyte commercial. Cute, huh? Amazing the things we'll promise when you need a few hours by yourself to recover from a night out. I guess Daddy didn't make it all the way to the commode.

That Nothing May Be Lost

The miracles of Jesus are a fascinating mix of healings, providing for the needs of people, defying or controlling nature, and raising people from death to life. The Bible records some of them, about forty in all. How many can you name?

Twenty-five of the miracles of Jesus are healings: the centurion's servant, the mother-in-law of Simon Peter, the ten lepers, the paralytic, the blind, the deaf, and others. There were eight exorcisms, three resurrections, Lazarus being a prime example. Ten involved His control of nature: Jesus walks on water, the miracle catch of fish, and Jesus calms the storm. The Gospel of Mark, the shortest of the four Gospels, records the most of Jesus's miracles. It is likely that far more miracles were performed than those we know and read about.

The Holy Gospel in church today was from John 6:1-15, "the Feeding of the Five Thousand." All four Gospels record this miracle about five thousand men, women, and children on the far shore of the Sea of Galilee. Most of the crowd had seen the miracle healings or had heard about them. They knew about Jesus's defiance of nature, and maybe witnessed an exorcism or two.

In the late afternoon, the people were hungry. Keeping up with Jesus was hard work. Jesus said to Philip, "Where shall we buy bread for all these people to eat?" John reports that Jesus was testing Philip and the other disciples. He already knew what He would do.

Philip's first response was that it would take ten months' salary to accomplish the task. Andrew, Simon Peter's brother, offered, "There's a small boy here who has five barley loaves and two fish." And then added, "But what are they among so many?" Jesus said, "Tell the people to sit down." The stage was set.

Jesus took the bread and the fish, gave thanks, and the food was distributed. When they all had enough to eat, the disciples collected the leftover pieces in baskets and filled twelve of them. Jesus had told them, "That nothing should be lost."

Don't know where the baskets came from? Don't know what happened to the leftovers? Maybe breakfast for the next day? The people said, "Surely this is the Prophet who is to come into the world."

Our pastor used this account as his sermon text. I didn't know that Christians had a number: the number twelve. Twelve Old Testament tribes of Israel. Twelve New Testament disciples. Twelve foundations and twelve gates for the New Jerusalem. Twelve baskets of leftover bread and fish.

John says that Jesus escaped the crowd and went to another mountain by Himself. How He pulled off that leave is also a mystery! A miracle?

Why the cleanup after all had eaten? An early environmentalist. Jesus simply said, "That nothing shall be wasted." I'll let you talk with your pastor or priest for the religious implications. Or maybe back to that number thing.

Consider the Louis Armstrong recording of "When the Saints Go Marching In" (May 13, 1938). The song is associated with the City of New Orleans. The NFL New Orleans Saints, a natural setting for the song. It originated as a Christian hymn, but is also played by jazz bands everywhere. It is part of the "folk song" and Black spirituals heritage of the early days of our country.

"Oh, when the saints, go marching in, Oh, when the saints go marching in, Oh, Lord, I want to be in that number, When the saints go marching in."[32]

Folks, we are not talking about marching into the Superdome. In this case, forgiven sinners, marching into heaven. Yes, I want to be in that number!

FYI:

1. Read about the New Jerusalem in Revelation 21.

2. The "Feeding of the Five Thousand" can be found in Matthew 14, Mark 6, Luke 9, and in John 3 (You might find John's account different and interesting). For another Bible search, find the account of Jesus feeding another crowd, this time four thousand. See the four Gospels.

That's the Ticket

An expression that I heard frequently from my mom was, "That's the ticket!" Usually that meant that a job was well done, an accomplishment of a child, other family member, or a friend.

In another story in this book, I reference the springtime Saturday morning preparation of six or more roosters, some for Sunday dinner and some for the freezer. Once beheaded, the chickens were dipped into scalding hot water for the removal of feathers. Mom demonstrated, and then my brother and I gave it a try. Picking the feathers off a scalded chicken was not an easy or quick task, but upon watching us do our best, she'd encourage us with the words, "That's the ticket!" The chickens were taken into the house where mom did the butchering.

Our dad had a huge potato patch between our house and the feed mill. When the Colorado potato beetle attacked the top of the ground green leaves of the root crop, he showed us how to knock those little bugs off the plants and into a small tin can with kerosene. Once the potato leaves had done their job and they dried, Dad dug each hill (row). Left to dry for a few days, we picked them up in baskets and deposited them on large shelves in our cool and rather dark basement. Potatoes kept rather well through the winter. So, Dad used the expression, too, in the gardens, at the mill, and at the house.

That's All Folks!

A TV commercial announces that we spend one-third of each day in bed. That assumes that those hours are spent sleeping. Some apparently don't need eight hours and do just fine on less. Some may go to bed at ten and get up at six, but find that sleep does not come automatically, the minute their head hits the pillow.

How do you put yourself to sleep? Count sheep? Maybe jumping over a water puddle or a fence? Count backwards from one hundred. From two hundred? Trying to recall your life in seventh grade? Remembering your high school years, your first date, your first car, or maybe your first trip out of the country? Maybe bedtime is prayer time, thanking God for your family, friends, and neighbors? Or thinking about what you'll have for breakfast, lunch, or dinner tomorrow? Maybe make your grocery list, mentally?

When I can't sleep, I try to think about stories I could write, especially if I'm just starting a new book. Last night was such an occasion.

I had written about thirty stories for this book. With such a nonsensical title, I often wondered whether people would buy it. So, this night, I focused on the "That" section.

First thought? Crazy or not, my initial thought was Daffy Duck. Maybe other comic characters ended cartoons with the "That's all folks" line, but Daffy is the one that I thought about.

Research in the morning told me that the line was first used in a 1930 Warner Brothers cartoon, spoken by the Bosco character. And that line may have been changed a bit from the line, "So long, folks," used at the end of some Bosco cartoons.

Porky Pig used the line too. Of course, he stuttered a little so it came out, "Th- th- th- that's all folks." But it was Daffy in "Porky's Duck Hunt" (April 17, 1937), his first appearance in Looney Tunes, that gets the credit.

Daffy was first paired with Speedy Gonzales, a character introduced a little later by Warner Brothers. Daffy appeared with other Looney Tunes characters, usually depicted as a foil for Bugs Bunny.

Creators and producers of Daffy Duck and the others were Tex Avery and Bob Clampett, all superseded by Mickey Mouse and Popeye cartoon characters.

A name that most of us associate with the Looney Tunes and Merrie Melodies cartoons is Mel Blanc (1937-1987), who did so many of the voices. Many may also remember the voice of Frank Gorshin, prominent in cartoon productions. We recall that Daffy Duck had a small speech problem, his extended mandible, causing a lateral lisp. Such creative "folks."

Dell Comics continued the popularity of Daffy Duck, Bugs Bunny, Porky Pig, and all of the other favorites that we loved. By the way, the grave marker epitaph for Mel Blanc: "That's all folks!"

And "the Other Thing" Section

Once Upon A Time.. 160

Everything Reminds Me of Something........................... 163

It's the Principle of the Thing................................. 166

Ben Grimm 168

The Thing 172

The Fly.. 173

The Blob 175

Mary, Mary, Quite Contrary 177

The Best Thing... 181

Pyrotechnics 184

It's the Real Thing.. 186

Pronouns and Other Irksome Things 187

Other Things All Too Common.................................. 189

Untucked 191

Now For the Really Weird 192

While We're At It 193

And "the Other Thing" Section

Bottled Water 195

Heaven or Hell? 197

Who Knew? 199

District Attorney or Defense Attorney? 202

And the Other Thing 204

One More Thing 206

Here's the Thing, and Then There's This 208

The Smash and Grab Thing 209

Extra! Extra! 212

Things That Happen In You 215

Something About A Sunday 220

Every Little Thing Is Gonna Be Alright 223

If It's Not One Thing, It's Another 225

Anything You Can Do I Can Do Better 228

Once Upon A Time

Moms, dads, grandparents, teachers, and little kids are all familiar with the expression, "Once upon a time." Fairy tales and nursery rhymes often begin with this line. Similar introductory lines might give everyone siting around a campfire an opportunity to join in the conversation. A dinner group during the coffee and dessert time often involves a sharing of personal stories on the topic for the day.

It's the "This one time, at band camp" thing when Michelle (Alyson Hannigan) comments to Jim (Jason Biggs) in the *American Pie* movie.

Elderly folks like to recall the days of yesteryear.

- "Once upon a time, I bought gasoline for nineteen cents a gallon."
- "Once upon a time, there were only three stations you could get on television."
- "Once upon a time, doctors made home visits to deliver a child or even to diagnose childhood disease and help to resolve discomfort and pain."
- "Once upon a time, the only water you drank was from the kitchen tap. Farm kids and others got their water from a brick-lined cistern in the backyard or a well that ran deep in the ground."

Once upon a time I watched late night TV. At the time, I thought David Letterman did a good job (and I was a Jay Leno fan, too). Often, Letterman on NBC (1982-1993) had a segment called "Is it anything?" He'd show a brief film clip of an off-beat event and ask his small audience, "Is it anything?" Sometime the answer was "Yes" and sometimes "No." It was rather stupid, but I liked that part of his show. Did my book begin in a New York City TV studio?

On an extremely cold and wintery night in 1990, my wife, daughter, son, and son-in-law went to Letterman's show. You had to get tickets (no cost) in the afternoon and then show up for the live show to be telecast at 10:30 p.m. in the central time zone. We were the last allowed to go in and get seats for that night.

I don't know if Letterman is to be credited with the use of the "thing" or not, but it makes sense to me. Isn't it funny the "things" you recall from decades ago? There's a small vignette involving a Safelight commercial in this book, much more recent, which also stuck in my mind. ("Who Knew?") Allow me to add a few "one time" things, all true:

- One time, with some CTC college guys, I was the pitcher in a fast-pitch softball game at the Nebraska State Penitentiary in Lincoln. Special rules: no base stealing, no intentional walks, and no hitting the batters. Don't remember who won. Maybe both teams? We played the inmates several times.
- One time, I had lunch atop the World Trade Center in NYC. I wish it was still there.
- One time, I spent a few late night hours at a Chicago police station. Four of us Cornhuskers had three six-packs of beer in the car, not one drop imbibed before being stopped by police.
- One time, in vocational agriculture shop class (Washington, Missouri), three of us Future Farmers of America were caught doing the Chubby Checker twist in back of the acetylene welding equipment.
- One time, I drove a school bus with fifty seventh and eighth grade kids from Boca Raton to Orlando (Disney World had opened recently). What was I thinking?!

- One time, several of us college guys drove from Nebraska to Kansas to celebrate a football win over Doane College. You could drink at age eighteen in Marysville. Now that I think of it, it may have happened more than once.
- One time, about age fifteen, three of us boys flew in a Piper Cub around St. Louis County, each of us allowed to "take the wheel" for about thirty seconds, with permission by our Baptist preacher pilot.
- One time, I served as probation officer of Riverview, Michigan, appointee of Judge Zitzelsberger. The judge was chairman of our congregation in Southgate, saw my fourth-year teacher salary, and figured I might need a little more cash. Boy, was he right!

So, here we go; the "Other Thing" section which I hope will remind you about many "things" in your rich and adventurous life?

Everything Reminds Me of Something

That's the title of a book by Adam Carolla, American comedian and actor, also known for radio and his very popular podcasts.

Barnes & Noble had just one copy of Carolla's book, which surprised me. He has written a half-dozen books. I thought the bookstore might have a few hundred on hand, and maybe even some paperbacks. I have written more books than Carolla and the major booksellers may or may not have even one copy of my books on the shelf (though they all say they'll order the title for you).

I saw a brief interview with Carolla on a morning cable news show. I thought that he and I might have similar views on many things, so I got the book. I was partly right and partly wrong about our similarities. His podcasts, current tours, and book are his opinions on questions (topics) that the folks ask him or send to him. His language is crude, and he mostly has the liberal slant. I was sorry to read that he is an atheist, an intriguing stance on life, liberty, and the pursuit of happiness.

Personal feelings aside, I made several observations:

1. My current book *This, That, and the Other Thing* reminds my readers of the many times we use the word "thing." Everything. Something. Anything. Nothing. Here's the thing. One more thing. And another thing, etc.

2. I agree with the thought in Carolla's title. Perhaps that's because I'm a trivia fanatic. When I'm not watching baseball or *Modern Marvels*, I'm tuning in to *Master Minds*, *The Chase*, and *Common Knowledge*. Maybe I can easily relate one thing with another because I was in Christian education for forty-five years (and teaching K-8 students).

Since my wife died, I've been an avid reader, mostly fiction. My eight published books included two novels, *Throw Me Something, Mister* and *Father Forgive Me, for I Have Sinned*.

3. I have trouble sleeping, though bedtime is usually near or later than midnight. On a recent sleepless night in New Orleans, I concentrated on one "thing," then tried to name any and all "things" related to that. Try it sometime. Nouns work best, but for a real challenge, try a verb (swim) or an adjective (angry). You'll be snoozing in ten!

Here are two noun examples:

1. Peanuts–Charlie Brown, Charles Shultz, George Washington Carver, Schroeder, Pig-Pen, Peppermint Patty, Woodstock, peanut brittle, peanut butter, Reese's, PB and J, Planters, Jiffy, Skippy, Tai food, peanut sauce, peanut buster parfait, peanuts and Cracker Jacks, baseball, boiled peanuts, throw the shells on the floor, peanut oil, goobers, pinders, ground nuts, monkey nuts, chocolate covered, Elvis's fried peanuts

2. Beaches–sand, sun, surf, sharks, some of the beaches I've enjoyed, Miami Beach, butter and banana, and too many more to mention, Zzzz, South Beach, Jones Beach, Sanibel and Captiva, Orange Beach, Gulf Shores, suntan, sunburn, sun block, sand crabs, sea turtles, sandpipers, oystercatchers, plovers, sea gulls, curlew, seashells, driftwood, swimsuits, bikinis, jellyfish, palm trees, cabanas, Snoop Dog, pelicans, beach erosion, Copacabana, Maui, Kawai, swim clubs, lifeguards, rip tides, the Olympics, red flags, beach

resorts, fishing piers, sun sets, sun rises, sea breeze, beach bars, beach weddings, beach volleyball, frisbees, sand bars, boogie boards

Some noun starters for you: potatoes, hot dogs, flowers, trees, toys, games, artists, comics, cars and trucks, mountains, lakes, candy bars, beer, wildlife, coffee, movies, music.

Give this a try tonight or sometime when you really need a nap.

FYI:

1. The Peanuts comic strip was published in seventy-five countries, in twenty-one languages, and in twenty-six hundred newspapers. It had a fifty-year run (1950-2000). Charles Shultz died in 2000, but re-runs continue today.

2. Peanuts are a major food crop, grown in tropical and subtropical climates. In the U.S., the states with major acreage include Alabama, Georgia, Florida, Mississippi, South Carolina, Texas, New Mexico, and Oklahoma. Thanks to a higher yield per acre, the U.S. produces 10 percent of the world crop on just 3 percent of world acreage.

3. China, India, Nigeria, and Sudan grow much of the rest in countries which export the crop. Mexico and Canada are major importers from the U.S.

4. A peanut is not a nut; it is a legume. Legumes supply nitrogen to the soil and include beans, vetches, clovers, and alfalfa. Legumes are one of the largest plant families in the world.

5. The Portuguese man o' war, not quite the same as the jellyfish, have powerful stings, which can kill fish, but rarely kill humans. Even dead or dying jellyfish washed up on shore can sting and burn your fingers and other limbs. Do not touch! You'll be sorry!

It's the Principle of the Thing

I don't have many worries, frustrations, or concerns that upset me, thank God! But I do have a dilemma once a month when I get a haircut.

I don't get $30 haircuts. For many years, I went to Super Cuts and, more recently, I go to Wonder Cuts. A few years ago, I could get a nice cut for $12 and leave a nice tip. In 2022, even the Wonder Cuts tab, with tip, is $20, depending on whether I get the senior discount.

The shop opens at 9:00 a.m. My stylist, as they like to be called, is Shannon. So, at about 8:45 a.m., I drive to the shop, park the truck, and wait at the door. No matter the weather, usually hot and humid, I like to be first in line.

The dilemma is that two or three other vehicles arrive before me, and, whether a man or a woman, the driver sits in the car until about 8:59 a.m. with the air conditioner working hard, perhaps having the last sips of their coffee, and listening to whatever. When one of the ladies unlocks the door and sets up a tripod announcing, "We're Open," there are three or four of us wanting to rush in, often wanting the same hair stylist as me.

Do I let one, two, or three folks in before I go in? There's an argument for that, sure, but I have enough Missouri mule in me to say, "No way, Jose!" I waited at the door, in uncomfortable heat, so I'm first to sign in. Wonder Cuts does not take reservations. The other two or three people have their own opinions about fairness. I convince myself. Hey, it's the principle of the thing!

It's the Principle of the Thing

Some friends and family think my middle name is Verbose. So, I'll skip the lengthy diatribe about resolving the dilemma to offer a secondary story using the principal of the thing for stories in the third sector of the book.

Anyone who has attended more than a few educator's conferences or conventions is familiar with this joke:

"Honey, get up. You'll be late for school."

From the bedroom: "I don't want to go to school today."

"Come on. We've been through this before. Up and at 'em."

"I think I have a sore throat."

"You think?"

"Must I go?"

"Yes, dear; you're the principal of the thing!"

In this case, the school is the "thing." In the earlier case, fairness is the "thing." You tell me: Am I first for the hair cut or not?

Do you have principles that you stick to vehemently? Do you have a principal who doesn't like school? Have you mastered the difference in spelling?

If you had (have) a principal who loves what he/she does and loves children, he's/she's your pal.

Get it?

Ben Grimm

I've never been into comic books. As a kid in the late 1940s, we did have some comic books at the house. I'm not sure who brought them or what happened to them. Recently, however, maybe because I've watched *The Big Bang Theory* a lot, I became interested in comic book history. In my first inquiries, I noted a fellow by the name of Ben Grimm, who some will recognize as The Thing. Aha! There must be a story here for my book!

Ben Grimm was the original tough guy in the Marvel universe, an ace pilot until exposed to intense cosmic radiation which caused the mutation in bodily appearance. Changed, he was now a rock-skinned monster with ominous super powers. Created by Stan Lee and artist Jack Kirby, Ben (The Thing) first appeared in The Fantastic Four #1 comic book (November 1961). I find myself wishing that Sheldon Cooper was sitting beside me to help in finishing this intro. Cooper and his friends from the TV show are comic book crazies!

Super heroes like The Flash, Wolverine, Wonder Woman, and the hundreds of others never piqued my interest, either. The real comic character enthusiasts love Comi-Con and go to that convention every year or plan to attend as many as possible. Not me! That desire comes way down my bucket list, just after a tractor pull in Salina, Kansas and the annual garlic festival in Gilroy, California.

Newspaper funny pages first appeared in our country mid-twentieth century. That section was the first one grabbed by the comics crowd when the newspaper hit the sidewalk or the lawn. Me? That section lay on the couch or the floor next to the finance and help wanted parts of the paper.

I think we got our first TV, black and white, about 1950. Professional basketball was broadcast more than baseball at the time. So, the paper we got, the *St. Louis Globe-Democrat*, regularly printed a blow-by-blow inning recap of the Cardinal's game the day or night before. I listened to every Cardinal broadcast on radio, but when they won, I'd read the game review anyway. I love my Red Birds!

Now, back to the funny pages.

There are many comic book/comic strip genres: super heroes, talking animals, western, romance, science fiction, and others. Comic publications began in our country in the early 1940s (*The Adventures of Obadiah Oldbuck*). The newspaper industry quickly recognized the need for a little fun, so numerous singles and strips vied for readers.

Superman comics launched the Golden Age of Comics. Then, a brief respite. And, in 1956, the Silver Age of Comics brought superheroes back. Superman, Spiderman, Batman, Wolverine, Wonder Woman, Green Lantern, Captain America, and others each had avid followers. Even without the superheroes, most adults can name a few comic book or strip characters.

Many of the characters also appear in feature films or short films shown between two movies in a theater: Bugs Bunny, Elmer Fudd, Donald Duck, and a dozen more were common. The Pink Panther, Roadrunner, Yosemite Sam, Pepé Le Pew, Foghorn Leghorn, Tweety Bird, Sylvester, etc. All were part of the comic scene after 1956.

Popular other singles included Garfield, Doonesbury, the Far Side, Peanuts Lil Abner, Krazy Kat, Pogo, B.C., Beetle Bailey, Blondie, and Family Circus also ring a bell in the memory of many. Less familiar to me were Liberty Meadows, Opus, Calvin and Hobbs, Zits, and Fox Trot.

As I'm writing about Ben Grimm (The Thing) in February 2022, America's disastrous failure in Afghanistan is in our daily news. Russia has close to 200,000 troops encircling Ukraine, claiming part of that sovereign nation to no longer being Ukraine.

Joe Biden's halting of the Keystone Pipeline on day one of his administration has resulted in our once energy independence being dependent, at least in part, on Vladimir Putin, the Saudi folks, and petroleum source elsewhere.

I drive a Ram 1500 truck. With a quarter tank left, it costs me $60 to fill. Predictions for $5 a gallon by summer are likely. Inflation is already soaring out of control. Our southern border is a sieve with illegal immigrants being flown by night anywhere in our country, often unannounced to the state officials. Violence rules many of our cities, both large and small. Elected Das turn violent criminals loose, believing that such social justice is somehow helpful. School children of every age are forced to wear masks for no apparent reason. The president is always looking detached from the people as he reads from a teleprompter. For the most part, he walks away from the media, not trusting himself to take questions.

I have friends who choose not to watch news programs any more. Maybe it's time I got into some comic books. Comic relief might be good right about now!

FYI:

1. Every state in our union hosts one or more Comi-Cons annually.

2. The first night telecast of Major League Baseball in our country was at Crosby Field, May 24, 1935, Cincinnati and Philadelphia.

3. The St. Louis Cardinals have won more World Series championships (eleven) than any other major league team, with the exception of the New York Yankees (seventeen). The Boston Red Sox are third (nine), the Brooklyn Los Angeles Dodgers are fourth (seven).

The Thing

Some of my readers might remember the movie, *The Thing* (1982). Kurt Russel and Wilford Brimley must have been between jobs at the time. They were two of the cast, part of a twelve-man research team in Antarctica. A parasitic alien being, fallen from space, had apparently been buried for one hundred thousand years. Oh, my God! Quite a stretch, don't you think? Can't you imagine the horror and havoc that the screen writers could create with that set-up?

In 2011, a re-make of *The Thing* appeared with a different cast. The film was a flop! But some will remember other science fiction movies produced about the same time such as *The Fly* and *The Blob*.

The Fly

My wife and I went to see this one when we lived in Detroit in the mid-1960s. Vincent Price was a main character in the original, which made it memorable to me. Barbara loved being scared to death in a movie. I mostly tried not looking at the big screen, feigning interest and even closing my eyes at times. That's how much I despise the sci-fi genre. Call me a scaredy cat if you must.

But horror films have a great following, certainly among the younger crowd. I have enough trouble getting to sleep as it is. I don't need any images of Freddie Kruger, Dracula, Hannibal Lector, aliens, predators, mass murderers, or ghosts in the closet or under the bed to keep me listening for strange sounds or leaving on a light in the bathroom.

In someone's list of one hundred scary movies, *The Thing* actually was #45 and *The Fly* was #68. I can watch Hitchcock's *Psycho*, but not *The Shining*. I'll watch *The Birds* with you, but not *Halloween* (either #1 or #2 on the list)!

The first Kubrick movie I watched was *2001-A Space Odyssey* and I'd watch it again (even by myself). I also saw *Full Metal Jacket* and *A Clockwork Orange*, neither of which kept me from sleeping well 'till dawn.

Now, back to *The Fly*. An experimenting with transportation of molecular matter. When a common house fly, unnoticed, enters the transportation device, things go horribly wrong. The mutation results in a grotesque and very large human fly. Makes your skin crawl, right? The 1986 remake with Beena Davies and Jeff Goldblum was a commercial success, netting $3,000,000 plus, produced on a budget of a half million. I don't recall seeing sequels *Return of the Fly* or *Curse of the Fly*. But I'll probably not see a common house fly as just a little pest that wants to sit on my potato salad while I'm sitting outside writing this story. Yuck! Did you ever study a little house fly up close and personal?

Oh, and Jack, whatever you do, don't go into Room 237!

The Blob

Really? People will actually pay good money to see a movie called *The Blob*? How do you define "blob," anyway? Are blobs dangerous, life-threatening, or seriously scary?

Some scary movie titles might raise the hairs on your neck or arms. At least, the title tells you what to expect. For example, *The Creature From the Black Lagoon*, *The Texas Chainsaw Massacre*, *The Exorcist*, *A Nightmare on Elm Street*, *The Blair Witch Project*, and *Night of the Living Dead*. How do these people sleep at night? Maybe they sleep during the day?

The Blob (1958) was Steve McQueen's feature film debut. What was he thinking? Auditions for that role might be risked if you didn't want to work at the shoe factory or pick grapes in the vineyards of California.

The plot? An alien entity crashes to Earth inside a meteorite. Okay, so far, so good. This lifeform consumes everything and everyone in its path, grows larger, redder, and more aggressive, larger than most buildings somewhere in Pennsylvania. At this point, you make sure that you've locked al the doors, double-checked all windows, and turned on lights in every room in the house.

The blob starts as a small jelly-like globule attached to an old man's hand. Okay, screenwriters, where could this lead? Hmm?

What? You have another scary prospect when you find a not-so-small dust bunny under that dresser that has not been moved or dusted since you moved into the house eleven years ago. And the dresser is in your bedroom? A puff of air from an open window propels the little creature and it is now resting on your bare ankle. You think that you saw an eye or part of a face in the dusty mass?

I don't know where the expression "letting your imagination run away with you" started, but the dust bunny is bravely fighting a not-so-little spider on a jelly-like blob, coming ever so close to your foot. Now what?

Mary, Mary, Quite Contrary

In rural Missouri in the 1930s and 1940s, family doctors often made house calls. My younger sister, Mary, two older brothers, one older sister, and I were all born in Lyon, delivered by Dr. Matthews whose office was in Beaufort, just a hop, skip, and a jump south on Highway P. Esther was the oldest (1933) and Mary the youngest (1945).

Our father was several years older than our mom. Etz, Howard, Gip, and I always thought that Mary was the favorite child. Truth be known, my dad sometimes called me "Itchie," rather than Rich, Richard, Ritchie, or even son. So, Dad may have thought of me and treated me as second favorite, but this story is about Mary.

Our parents were not the strictest mom and dad, but we learned respect for them and seldom got scolded or disciplined harshly or inappropriately. Certainly there were some spankings, but I don't remember any of them or the reasons for them. We had no disparaging feelings for our mom and pop, and I don't recall any sit-downs or heart-to-heart talks to get us back on the right track.

Our closest barber shop was in Washington, Missouri, only a fifteen-minute drive to town. A neighbor, Adolph Werner, just walking distance from our house, cut my brother's hair and mine. I guess Mary may have gotten a trim in town or with scissors and mom or Esther?

Mom cut Dad's hair and did his once-a-week shave in preparation for church on Sunday. That ritual brings to mind the thirty-inch long barber's strap that hung close to the bathroom, had indoor plumbing. The strap was well-worn leather, about three inches wide, used for sharpening the straight razor, mom's shaving tool. It was also used occasionally, though sparingly for disciplining the kids. Or some of them.

Mary told us that she was spanked once. Like the rest of us, she can't remember the specifics, but it happened one Sunday after church. Our mom and dad took church seriously!

Howard remembered a time when he got the strap as a very young child, apparently at the breakfast table. Reportedly, he peed on Dad's pancakes when spanked. No one can confirm the said incident. Maybe Howard was acting up in church, as well?

No doubt you were reminded of the nursery rhyme "Mary, Mary, Quite Contrary" upon seeing the title of this story. Well, me, too.

"Mary, Mary, quite contrary,
How does your garden grow?
With silver bells and cockle shells
And pretty maids all in a row."

The origin of the nursery rhyme is said to be uncertain. The character (Mary) is most often a reference to Mary Tudor (Bloody Mary), the first daughter of Henry VIII. That daughter later became Queen Mary!

An earlier version begins, "Mistress Mary" and it dates back to 1744. Some say Mary referees to Mary Queen of Scots. Catholic historians suggest that the "silver bells" might be the Sanctus or altar bells?

Mary, Mary, Quite Contrary

Cockle shells are edible marine bivalve mollusks, perhaps found in North Atlantic waters of the English coast?

Back in Missouri for a moment, a cockle was a thorny weed which stuck to your pant legs, socks, or shoes until you physically removed them one at a time. But that, of course, has no relevance to seafood, seashells, or Mary Queen of Scots.

Pretty maids all in a row? Other than the obvious, not a clue!

On our small property in Lyon, there were gardens everywhere: a half-acre potato patch stretching between the gravel driveway and the feed mill, another half-acre for sweet corn across the road by the Deppermanns, a large plot on the southside of the house for radish, carrots, green beans, tomatoes, cucumbers between the front yard and the fence for the cow pasture. We boys were always the forced labor for crop prep, crop cultivation, and harvesting.

Mary stayed in the house, maybe playing or just watching mom. What's up with that? Oh, and cutting the grass on the front yard and back lawns, in the ditches next to the highway, pulling weeds? Even the spring chicken butchering on a Saturday morning, Mary was a spectator, not a farmhand, getting dusty, dirty, and sweaty.

But, you know, we love our little sister. Mary followed me to Concordia Teacher's College in Nebraska, graduated with a B.S. in Education (1966), and later got a Master's Degree from Nebraska in Lincoln. One year of teaching in Big Rapids, Michigan, then both teaching and administration in Nebraska and Colorado. Her forty-four years of elementary education was an example for her daughter, Jennifer, a second grade teacher in Grand Junction, and grandchild, Kate, soon to graduate from Arizona State in Tucson.

I realize I could have chosen a different nursery rhyme for this story. Maybe "Mary Had A Little Lamb," but we boys likely would be the caretakers of the "fleece as white as snow" lamb or sheep anyway. Little sisters. You can't live with 'em and you can't live without 'em!

The Best Thing

Christmas traditions. Every family has them. This story is about a tradition that my sister and her husband began some years ago in Grand Junction, Colorado. It involves Christmas cash for the grandkids, and secret hiding places for the money, which, when found, is shared equally by each.

Christmas traditions tend to relate to the Christmas tree, Christmas presents, Christmas food, and Christmas lights and decorations.

The tree? Real or artificial? Small, medium, or large? When to put up the tree? When to take down the tree? Ornaments, ribbons, tinsel and/or snow, and the item on top of the tree?

Everyone does their own "thing."

The presents? I like that word rather than gifts. I guess there's really no difference. When to open the "things" under the tree? Open one at a time, or just have a huge flurry of ripped wrappings, exclamations of "thank yous", and an embarrassing pile of debris? The trash guys must love the first pick-up day after the Christmas presents.

The food? This starts sometime right after Thanksgiving with making Christmas cookies, candy or caramel apples, fruit cake, etc. And what to eat on Christmas Eve or Christmas day?

Christmas lights and decorations? Inside the house and outside? Go small, with lights on the tree and a few candles or other lighting inside? Go large, for the Clark Griswold effect, causing the electric meter to race toward a utility bill that gets paid over a couple of month?

Other traditions at the most wonderful time of the year revolves around Christmas worship, special programs or concerts, family travel. Wreaths and holiday greenery, Christmas drinks and parties, Christmas movies, and the list goes on. Advent calendars, Christmas caroling, Christmas cards.

My sister's tradition is to place cash somewhere in or near the house, hopefully not found easily. It is the last Christmas thing when all other presents have been opened. Clues to the location of cash might be given for days before the big day. Maybe save the clues for family time on Christmas Eve or Christmas day.

One year the cash was deposited in the fingers of Christmas gloves. Another, hidden on top of a ceiling fan, maybe not needed for comfort in Grand Junction in late December. Another time, the loot was placed inside the wrapper of a Million Dollar candy bar, part of a centerpiece in the kitchen. Maybe you have to be a teacher to be that inventive with cash and clues?

Whether tradition or just of necessity, my family in East Central Missouri always chopped a cedar tree from nearby hillsides or cow pastures. Our large front room was not heated in our winter months, but it was heated for Christmas Eve and Christmas day. Eggnog was a once-a-year thing we drink that I never really liked as a kid or as an adult. A highball may have been served at times Wine was never a part of our Christmas celebration, even for the several special meals. Our presents as kids tended to be the frugal and functional variety. Whatever the year, Christmas was always special, no matter how memorable the presents.

Maybe you would like to try this tradition at your house. How about the following:

- under a dinner plate on Christmas day?
- inside the bottom section of the family snowman?
- in the mailbox in a homemade Christmas card for the kids?
- tucked into one of the several poinsettia plants in the house?
- hidden in a match box near the Christmas candles?
- at the bottom of the cookie jar under a napkin?
- tied to one of the several trees in the front or the backyard?
- taped under the chair at the Christmas table?
- a really "green" bundle at the top of the Christmas tree?
- under the welcome mat at the front door?
- inside the kids' pillow cases?
- on the door of the ice box?
- inside the pages of the Bible? Luke 2?
- in a plastic Easter egg in the backyard after a nice snow?
- in the pages of the kids' required reading during the Christmas break?

Pyrotechnics

Pyrotechnics (from the Greek, pyr [fire] and technikos [made by art]), is a "thing" and much more than most people think or know. It is the science of creating fireworks. In Lyon, Missouri in the 1950s, we just called them firecrackers, seen only on the Fourth of July.

We normally associate fireworks with the Fourth of July, our Independence Day, but New Year's Eve gets its share of pyrotechnics, too, not just in our country, but the world over. Who has not watched the fireworks display in Times Square and other major locations in the world?

Our rural Missouri Fourth of July had a little fire and smoke, but not much of a show. If you or a big brother happened to go into town to buy a few firecrackers, that likely included some sparklers, some one-and-a-half inch firecrackers, and possibly a cherry bomb or two. If a neighbor spent a little more, some Roman candles or other rocketry might have also lighted the sky once darkness set in.

Our house on Highway P was a two story: two bedrooms upstairs, an attic, and a not-to-be-trusted porch that we thought might fall into the backyard if too much weight was put on it. That screened-in porch allowed us to look to the northeast, to Washington, about fifteen miles away, to hear the sounds of explosives and maybe see a few sparking fires of various colors, but I don't ever recall going to the big city of about 10,000 to see the pyrotechnics.

Pyrotechnics

More than you might think? Yes, besides being used for parts of automobile air bags, making safety matches, oxygen candles, explosive bolts and other fasteners, and applications for mining, quarrying, and demolition, there are nearly twenty categories of fireworks, a few of them being: air bust, binary powders, comet or meteor, mine, smoke pots, concussion, falls, and fireballs; the concussion type maybe the most recognizable?

The music industry, especially for outdoor concerts and major performances of rappers and others, employ pyrotechnics for effect. Most MLB parks have pyrotechnics, especially after home runs are hit and after a winning game.

The major producers of pyrotechnics in the U.S. include the 130-year-old Zambelli Group (Warrendale, Pennsylvania), Wholesale Fireworks (Hubbard, Ohio), Atomic Fireworks Wholesale (Seabrook, New Hampshire), Galaxy Fireworks (various locations in Florida), and large businesses in Alabama, New York, Virginia, and Missouri.

Pyro Spectaculars in Rialto, California produces many firecracker shows.

Among leading producers in the world, Brooks in London, Fantastic Pepperstock in England, Star in the UK, Maravillas in Colombia, Standard in India, and two in China, Liuyang and Grand Dragon.

Happy Fourth of July and Happy New Year!

It's the Real Thing

The Coca-Cola and Pepsi war has been the subject of TV specials since the soft drink industry began, Coke about twelve years on the market before Pepsi.

Keeping with the theme of this section of the book and whether it is or is not a "thing," do you remember the jingle that accompanied the Coke commercials? "Coca-Cola, it's the real thing!" Coke was created by a pharmacist, John Pemberton, in Columbus, initially as a medication.

The best-selling soft drinks in more than one ranking I've seen include Coca-Cola (#1), Pepsi (#2), and these: Fanta, Diet Coke, Mountain Dew, Sprite, Diet Pepsi, Coke Zero, and Diet Mountain Dew. 7-Up is enjoyed in many lands. Schweppes is on most grocery shelves, especially liked in Switzerland. Blue Sky is popular in France. One unfamiliar to me is Moxie. Appletiser is a common choice in the Union of South Africa.

Some coffees make the soft drink category. Nescafe in Switzerland and Folgers in the U.S. Gatorade is big in our country; Red Bull is big in Austria. The Germans like Sprite and Fanta.

Pronouns and Other Irksome Things

One of my pet peeves is the incorrect use of pronouns, chief among them, the use of I and me. People you regard as well-educated, and well-known personalities, misuse these regularly.

"Your mom brought presents for you and I."

"That story was about her and I."

"It would not shock him or I if it didn't sell."

I'll put on my teacher's hat for a moment. In the first example above, the pronouns are subjects of the preposition "for." You would not say "brought presents for you and I." You'd correctly say, "brought presents for you and me."

Similarly, in the second, the preposition is "about." So, "That story is about her and I," is wrong. It should read, "That story is about her and me." Her and I are subjective pronouns; her and me are objective pronouns.

In the third, "you and I" are direct objects. It just sounds wrong to say, "would not shock him or I." So, don't say "him or I." He and I are subjective; him and me are objective.

Listen carefully to any ten minutes of your favorite news show. A host or one of the guests will use pronouns incorrectly and unknowingly.

It's basic grammar folks! "Join Dan and I in ten minutes for full details." Or "Us and a few others will return for our opinions." Wrong! Wrong! Wrong!

Okay, so I'm on a roll. How about the expression, "You know"? Perhaps heard mostly from athletes, but it's so commonly said. When asked about the ball game yesterday, having been shut out on Monday, but having scored eleven runs on Tuesday, the shortstop explains:

"Well, you know, pitching is the name of the game. Our guy, you know, was on fire, you know. His curveball was a winner, you know, and with ten strike-outs in five innings, you know, one or two runs would win the game, you know. We scored lots of runs, and that's what we did, you know, tonight."

Such explanations are often given in choppy replies, fluent language not a real strength in the dugout.

Are you as bothered by other commonly said words as I am? Words like "I mean" and "Just sayin'"? How about "that said" or "at the end of the day?" Really? Just before I go to bed, "long after midnight."

When you submit a manuscript for publication, a good editor of your writing will catch those subjective and objective pronoun misuses. For those other irksome expressions, we might just have to put up with them, you know?

I could go on for ten more pages if all the transgendered things (pronouns) were part of this diatribe, but I'll spare you my conservative and not-very-woke slant on that. Just sayin'!

Other Things All Too Common

My notice of irksome expressions didn't begin when I started writing and publishing books, which was quite recent. Here's an example from a classmate in the mid-1950s, at a one-room school in Campbellton, Missouri.

In the fifth grade, when told something that might be questionable or not true, a boy named Keith would exclaim, "I ain't done it!" The intended meaning, of course, was "I don't believe you" or "I doubt that." Now, Keith may not have been the brightest light on the Christmas tree, but even his use of "ain't" was years before the word was found in any dictionary or part of modern lexicon.

You've heard all of the following:

1. "Gotcha"
2. "Just sayin"
3. "It is what it is"
4. "Tell me about it"
5. "You're kidding me"

"It is what it is." Sounds like checking with Bill Clinton would be the right source for truth here. Of course, it is what it is. Otherwise I would not have said it! You agree with me then, right? Similarly, "Just saying" (often shortened to "just sayin'") sounds a bit apologetic. It's unnecessary! You don't have to justify what you just said!

"You're kidding me" is usually said as a question. But you just said it, and I guess you meant what you said. It's not that unbelievable, though the person you're talking with doubts you. You were 100 percent certain, so you often follow with, "No, really!" or "I kid you not."

When someone tells you, "Gotcha!" it's their way of telling you "I get it" or "I understand" or "Yes, that's right!" The longer expression, also overused, "I hear what you're saying."

The PC crowd, and in this case, maybe the non-Christian folks, object to "Merry Christmas." So, when you tell them "Merry Christmas," they might say, "Happy holidays." And you might want to follow with, "No, I meant Christmas, not the days just before the December 25 or the days that follow." There are a lot of holidays each year, but on July 3 and July 5, we don't say "Happy holidays." The same for Labor Day, President's Day, Easter, etc.

Your neighbor says she's really tired of all of the cold weather. You agree with her as you are ready for spring and summer. You mention an approaching cold air blast out of Canada and you say, "Another four or five days of freezing temperatures." She says, "Tell me about it." You want to yell back at her, "I just told you about it! Shall I say it again?!"

Untucked

Untucked is a relatively new casual men's (and now women's) apparel business, established in 2011, headquartered in New York City. Stores were opened in Chicago, Los Angeles, San Francisco, and Austin, the first brick-and-mortar shop in Soho, New York in September 2015.

Seventy-four stores now sell the Untucked apparel in the U.S., UK, and Canada. The most popular items sold are men's shirts, cut a bit shorter than typical shirts, meant not to be tucked into the pants.

Untucked is a "thing" and a somewhat expensive thing. Flannel Henleys go for $89, heavyweight polos from $75 to $85, and long sleeve tees about $50. Jackets and other apparel are available at most stores. Skirts and dresses for the ladies are showing up in many of the stores with similar costs.

I grew up in the church and often saw loose-fitting shirts worn by many pastors and district executives. These tended to be popular for casual wear, the down front fabric often covering the midsection and worn untucked. I find myself wanting to ask the originators of Untucked if the trend started in the church.

May we always have entrepreneurs who come up with new "things" that are popular with the public.

Now For the Really Weird

What would a book that asks the question "Is it a thing?" be if it contained no reference to Bigfoot, commonly also referred to as Sasquatch, especially in Canada?

The ape-like creature, purported to inhabit the forests of North America, is a "thing" to many, but the majority of mainstream scientists prefer to say that the Bigfoot stories are due to regional folklore and misidentification.

Evidence supporting the existence of such a creature include casts of larger-than-life footprints, visual sightings, video and audio recordings, photographs, etc. Some of these are known to be hoaxes. Bigfoot is an icon with the fringe subculture of cryptozoology.

You've heard of some of the other regional names for such creatures: the skunk ape (Florida), the Yeti (Asia), the Yowie (Australia), all ingrained in the cultures of their region. Some lesser known creatures include the Grassman (Ohio), Fouke Monster (Louisiana), and Wood Booger (Virginia). There are stories of Bigfoot creatures in New York, Missouri, Michigan, Arizona, and Illinois.

With so many reported sightings, you might want to check under your bed tonight before dozing-off: Mattress Man, Pillow Papa, Dust Bunny Daddy, and Cousin Bogey Man may make an appearance.

While We're At It

I've never watched any of the paranormal programs that I see as I browse the internet. I have absolutely no interest in them. And I don't think that's because I'm scared to watch them.

Without disparaging anyone who has lost a loved one or a friend in an accident on our roads and highways, I'm amused (sorry, could not think of a better word) at the roadside crosses I see as I travel everywhere. Most of these are not very elaborate, and for good reason, I suppose. A few get very carried away and "decorate" the site with all manner of lights, mirrors, flowers, and personal remembrances. I'm surprised that the DOT and other agencies allow the practice, yet I understand the sentiment. There are more appropriate ways to honor or remember those lost to automobile accidents.

Don't ghosts and apparitions have a negative, even an evil, connotation? Okay, a life or lives was (were) lost at the site. Wouldn't their spirit prefer to hang at the place where the body was buried or where their ashes were scattered?

I have not studied the New Testament Book of Revelation much, but with that possible exception, I don't find much about ghosts and other paranormal entities in the scriptures. Jesus appeared at and after His resurrection many times, but those were real happenings, not apparitions. Jesus did not appear as a ghost. Have you ever thought of Jesus as a scary being?

I lay on our bed, holding my wife's hand as she took her last breaths. So far, her spirit has not reappeared in any form at the house, though her ashes are in an urn rests at the foot of the bed. I believe her spirit did appear in heaven on that night when she died, so that begs the question: Are there ghosts in heaven? And what about on the last day, our resurrection? The body and soul reunite, as they were on Earth? As they are in heaven as paranormals?

Bottled Water

My father could have been the poster dad for "old school" if that expression had been used in the 1950s, Here's an example:

While watching the *Ed Sullivan* TV show one Sunday evening (black and white, of course), a man was balancing a dozen ceramic plates or saucers on the top of a dozen five-foot poles on stage. He started all of the saucers spinning and kept them all spinning for approximately one minute, not one of them falling to the floor. Quite a feat, right?

As several of us kids, and maybe even our mom, explained the success of his entertaining act, Dad said to us, "Just pictures, kids. Just pictures." In other words, "That's not really happening. There must be some trick with that."

What would my dad think or say if he saw what's happening today with all of the modern technology? My dad was considerably older than my mom. He died when I was in the early years of high school.

Take the telephone. At our house in Lyon, Missouri, the phone was a large, wooden box that hung on the wall. To call someone, you would ring the phone operator with a ring or two by turning the handle on the top of the box. The operator would then ring the party you wanted to talk to. About a dozen people (families) were on the same party line. I think our "number" was three long rings and a short one. What a difference a "day" makes!

Now, take the plastic water bottle that everyone in America today uses and drinks from. Back home, the only water we had was from the kitchen faucet or a water hose. While there is still a lot of uses of water from the tap in the kitchen, most families today buy and use some or a lot of bottled water. If Dad saw that our bottled water came from Texas (Ozarka), he'd exclaim, "No way!"

I live by myself and don't have many visitors at the house, either family or friends. After Hurricane Ida hit less than two months ago as of this writing, I saved all of the plastic bottles and aluminum cans I've used, the parish having canceled or suspended pick up of recyclables because of lack of staff. In my carport, I have eleven large bags full of aluminum and plastic. Metals and paper products (newspapers, too), for some reason, is no longer collected by my waste management company.

Prices of just about everything have increased, but at the major stores like Costco and Sam's Club, bottled water is still fairly inexpensive. Of course, back home, we didn't have to budget for water expense.

Space travel? A few earthlings have traveled into space and returned to Earth safely. Those who can afford the very expensive travel to space will continue to do that for decades. Just pictures though, right?

Heaven or Hell?

It might take quite an effort to convince an atheist and others who have never had a faith life that there is a heaven and a hell. Talking, by itself, would not accomplish this. Maybe a life-ending or life-changing experience would help?

As for me and my house, yes, there is a heaven! Heaven is a THING! As for me and my house, yes, there is a hell. Hell is a THING! Simple explanation, of course. And the pictures of our description of both are surely accurate. Even unbelievers have a perception of the two. Heaven is beautiful. Hell is not pretty!

I do not quote scriptures in the effort to justify my belief. Heaven knows (and hell knows, too) the references to both. People believe what they want to believe, but I will state my case for the defense.

I believe in Jesus, who lived, was crucified, died, and was buried.

I believe that Jesus descended into hell. What a spectacular experience that must have been! I believe Jesus rose from death, ascended into heaven, and sits there with the Father, to return to this earth and bring believers to eternal life in heaven.

I believe in the Holy Spirit, the Lord and Giver of life. Together with the Father and the Son, the Spirit is worshiped and glorified.

Eternal life is hard to comprehend. But living with the Trinity in heaven or living with the devil is not a difficult decision.

And here is the "other thing": Believers live eternally with God purely by His grace. Nothing we can do earns our spot in heaven. The Holy Spirit brings us to faith and keeps us in that faith. As I have taught for forty-five years in Christian schools across this country: There will be a lot of bad sinful people in heaven, and a lot of good (sinful) people in hell. And there's an abundance of scripture to verify that.

Sola Scriptura! Sola fide! Sola gratia!

Billy Graham fans or not, check out "heavenornot.net" on the internet.

Who Knew?

After deciding on the title for this book, I began to make notes for topics and titles to be included for each of the three sections: This, That, the Other Thing. I quickly discovered the many times each day when I used or heard the word "thing."

I wondered, for example, what are the "things" in life that we could call really personal? Uniquely mine? Special to me?

Maybe your car or truck? Your pillow? Your place to relax? Maybe a special hat or other clothing or accessory? Your BFF? (I think "Best" is limited to one).

In the offseason for baseball, I find a few TV shows that are entertaining. One of those I like is *Beat Bobby Flay* on the Food Channel. After two chefs prepare a dish, using an item that Flay chooses as the "thing" that must be the star of their dish, the winner names a dish that is called their "signature" dish. The majority of the show then shows the cooking contest between the two. Flay often wins, even though the other chef has likely prepared that dish hundreds of times. Flay has limited knowledge of the dish and perhaps has never prepared it.

So, that is a lengthy introduction to this story, which is not about food at all. This is a story about drive-by shootings.

Most of us are familiar with drive-ins, whether the nearly forgotten drive-in outdoor movie theaters or the ubiquitous drive-in diners or restaurants. Then there's the drive-up and drive-thru businesses like banks, pharmacies, and fast-food restaurants.

Before the self-serve gas stations got wise and sophisticated enough to make the customer pay for fuel before pumping it, there was the drive-off (pull-up, put in as much fuel as you thought you could get away with, and quickly drive away without paying). I suspect that most drive-offs were never apprehended.

Now, the drive-by. A drive-by shooting is firing a weapon from a moving vehicle. The shooting might result from a road rage incident or many other circumstances. The shooting may involve firing into a vehicle, into a business, or into a crowd or a gathering of sorts.

Those who pay attention to national and/or local news may think that drive-by shootings are a recent happening ("thing"). Actually, most sources name Nestor Makhno, commander of the Revolutionary Insurrectionary Army of Ukraine, as performing the first drive-by using horse and carriage with a machine gun to quickly assault targets and flee.

Griselda Blanco, a drug lord of the 1970-80s, is reported to have done motorcycle drive-bys in Miami.

In Chicago, Bugs Moran is known for his Tommy Gun assaults versus Al Capone, again, some years ago.

There are similar drive-by reports from the Mexican Mafia (1992) and from Philadelphia (1993).

Various hip-hop artists were targeted by drive-by shootings (Tupac Shakur, B.G., and others) all made national headlines.

California, Texas, Florida, Illinois, and Washington are reported as states with the most drive-by shootings (The Progressive New Science, Violence Policies Center).[33]

I've lived in New Orleans for thirty-plus years and drive-by shootings have become almost routine. Injuries and/or deaths have often resulted among innocent bystanders, including young children, either in vehicles with adults or in a residence. Though I haven't researched it, I've wondered if drive-by shootings are a "thing" in Norway, Brazil, Kenya, Russia, or France? Certainly such violence is not a "thing" only in the U.S. Or is it?

A Safelite commercial, often seen on TV, shows a young woman who, like most of us, cannot do without her car. She gets a crack in her windshield and needs it fixed and fixed quickly. She says, "My car is not just for wheels, it's my after-work decompression zone." She contacts Safelite and finds that they have exclusive technology to repair or replace the windshield, either at their shop or even out on the road. The commercial ends with the woman saying, "Who knew it (Safelite technology) was a thing?"

Who knew drive-by shootings was (is) a thing? As 2022 begins, more and more people are discovering that such are real. In New Orleans, there were 220 homicides reported in 2021.[34] The first homicide of the new year in the Big Easy was a twelve-year-old boy, shot and killed and left at the side of the road. A six-year-old girl was shot one day later in a car with her mother and another child, neither of which was critically injured. Who knew? Maybe the better question is, who cares? Based on the random injuries and/or deaths that occur, it is obvious that the shooters don't!

District Attorney or Defense Attorney?

My understanding of the job of a district attorney is to receive police reports and decide whether to prosecute criminal offenses or not.

In New York City January 2022, the DA decided to define criminal offense in very narrow terms. He publicly stated that many offenses prosecuted in the past would no longer be regarded as criminal. Among those would be marijuana usage and sale, prostitution, trespassing, turnstile jumping, and resisting arrest. His conclusion drawn from other police statements was that no criminal act should be punished by more than a twenty-year incarceration. Even armed robbery, if no shots were fired, would be treated with leniency. Oh, my God!

Let's start with the easy one: jumping a turnstile. I lived in New York City in the 1990s and occasionally had to or chose to take a subway. I never saw anyone skip the fee and jump a turnstile. But let's say that 50 percent of that subway traffic jump the turnstile or ride the train without cost.

Some folks are too heavy to accomplish that jump. Some ladies, not in pants, may feel very embarrassed to attempt a jump. Some folks believe it only right to pay for the transportation. What would result from that loss of revenue? Maintenance of the system and payment of subway personnel would suffer drastically. Soon, no one would want to rely on the service. What about those who regularly take a taxi or a bus? Refuse to pay and still use bus service?

What about trespassing? You own or rent a property (house, apartment, office, etc.) and you do your best to keep it in good condition. So, one day, some guys set up tents on your site and sell jewelry, clothing, or other goods at discounted costs. Trespassing is no longer criminal and you can do nothing to move the squatters out. You would vote for that DA the next time he/she runs for office.

Resisting arrest? Isn't that what happened in Ferguson, Baton Rouge, Baltimore, New York City, and other locales with famous news stories? We have seen in the last decade or so what happens when people attempt to escape the law. If you can outrun the law officer(s) or have help in such an escape, your community would crumble into certain chaos very quickly.

Weave the marijuana and prostitution offenses into your consideration. The possibilities for decay and degradation are obvious. With so many communities in our country having already defunded police departments, imagine how much farther "soft on crime" policies would demoralize law enforcement. Is the ultimate goal of such liberal thinking to eliminate policing?

Inconceivable!

A new mayor, Eric Adams, took office in New York City at the start of 2022. It seemed that he would attempt to make the city safe again. A few months later, together with his DA who was more interested in defending criminals, our largest city will, once more, be less safe for the law-abiding citizens. It's not a place that I want to visit, and certainly not a place where I want to live.

And the Other Thing

What this book needs is a little more baseball, right?

My friend in Carolina likes to kid me about many things: my garage sale treasures, my many trees, shrubs, and flowering plants, and more than any-THING, my love for baseball. Watching a nine-inning baseball game, for him, is like watching paint dry or watching grass grow. My response to him is that he has no appreciation for the intricacies and nuance of the game, America's game. One of those rarely called "things" in a ballgame is the balk.

A balk is called by any of the four umpires in major league, minor league, or earlier stages of playing the game. It is called on the pitcher and only when there is one or more runners on base, no matter how many outs in the half-inning. When a balk is called, the one or more base runners get to advance automatically one base–second, third, or home.

The simple definition of a balk might be stated like this: anything the pitcher does, with the foot on the pitching rubber, to deceive the base runner(s). That could be something as simple as dropping the baseball from the glove, slight movement when in the stretch or full windup, not throwing to first base without stepping off the rubber, kicking (pointing) your front leg at an angle somewhere between or toward home plate or first base, etc. Yeah, I know. If you're not into baseball, that may be confusing. If you know the game and the rules of the game, however, you'll likely call balk at the same time as an umpire calls it.

And the Other Thing

Is a balk a "thing"? You bet your metal cleats, it is! A balk can be the difference in scoring a run or not, winning a game if called in the last of the ninth in a tie game, and more.

When my family moved from South Texas to New Orleans in 2000, I trained with the New Orleans Umpire Association and did ballgames either as the plate umpire or on the bases for all ages of playground ball, high school, and ladies' and men's softball, fast pitch or slow pitch. It only paid $20 a game, but I thoroughly enjoyed being the game official.

The last summer (season) I did games, the association treasurer, Mr. Joe, asked me if I could suspend payment in lieu of paying other guys who needed the money a lot more than I did. I agreed. Mr. Joe ran off with the association's cash, paid by the teams and playgrounds, following Hurricane Katrina in 2005. I was owed about $1,500 at the time, having worked four or five nights a week and on weekends. I and others were never paid for the games owed us.

You want a really interesting umpire's call? Check out the infield fly rule sometime on the internet. Nuance? To someone who is not a baseball fan, plan for a minimum of thirty minutes and a baseball diamond drawing or two to learn the rule. Or, hey, just forget it. I can explain it to you in five minutes or less. It's a good rule, both for the offense and the defense.

One More Thing

A busy mother, rushing to get the kids to school and trying not to be late for her job, hustles everyone to the family van, hoping that the kids have not forgotten something.

"I'm disappointed in you guys," she says, as four car doors slam shut. "Tommy, I told you two days ago to clean the cat litter box. It's still a smelly mess. Tiff, the dishes have not been put away. You clean the sink and empty the dishwasher first thing when you get home today!" The youngest, Steven, can't imagine what's coming next. "Stevie, you're only six, but Dad told you Sunday to put all of your games and toys where they belong. I nearly tripped on your stuff this morning. That's your job before Dad gets home tonight. One more thing, and this is for all three of you. Dirty clothes go to the laundry room every day. Do not wait till Dad or I have to remind you, okay?"

Switch it to a high school classroom situation with seniors.

"Class, many of you will go off to college in less than three months, but I continue to still see mistakes in grammar. Your English teachers will wonder what kind of teacher you had in high school."

"Miss Miller," they say, almost in unison, "everyone makes mistakes. We're not perfect."

"The thing is," Miss Miller explains, "your instructors in college won't be nearly as patient with you as I have been. If an assignment is due on the tenth, get it done before the tenth! Before you turn in your writing, check for errors. Proofread! Paragraphing has been stressed all year. Subject and verb agreement, right? Objective pronouns are always problematic."

"Okay, okay, okay! We got this," her students almost shout. "Is that everything?"

"One more thing. Computers don't catch everything. You check spelling and punctuation."

Most of the class stopped listening minutes ago.

I frequently watch "The Five" on Fox News late in the afternoon. One of the five persons on the show, with only a few minutes left for the hour, announces, "Next, one more thing." So, everyone, as time allows after a commercial or two, has chosen a parting "thing" to end the show. Most of the five are politically right, but the "one more thing" items are usually without a political bent.

Here's the Thing, and Then There's This

Whether in a monologue or participating in a discussion with others, someone will say to make their point, "Here's the thing." This might be to make a final point or in an effort to end discussion. It's a way to wrap up a topic; one last comment.

Either of the two phrases in the title above might be used in debating the value of cryptocurrency (Ethereum, Cardano, Solano, Tethm, or others). Positives of mentioned cryptocurrency are "It's a digital form of money that anyone can use," "It's virtually immune from governmental interference and counterfeiting," or "It has great potential for profit." However, one cautions others, "And there's this; the IRS treats crypto as property for federal income tax purposes."

Bitcoin is one of the most common cryptocurrencies as it has grown by leaps and bounds in recent years, as much as 12,000 percent in value. Ten thousand in bitcoin a decade ago might be valued in the millions today!

When discussing COVID vaccinations, proponents of vaccines might tout a half-dozen reasons to be vaccinated, including the use in (on) children as young as three or four. But another might interject: "And then there's this, it's not known how the vaccines of the very young might affect boys and girls in later life." There are other howevers, both practical and political.

The Smash and Grab Thing

A quote from the December 2021, AMAC Magazine is an apt introduction to this item. By Robert B Charles, it is titled "A Tidal Wave of Crime Floods America."

Charles wrote, "Some will say 'Crime ebbs and flows,' and that is true. But just as tides rise and fall in response to known factors, crime waves come and go as a result of identifiable factors. The key is reducing what promotes crime and improving what prevents, deters, and responds to it."[35] Smash and grab crime occurred routinely in 2021, with plenty of videos to prove it. Gangs (groups) of marauders selected a prime site, set a time for the robbery, smashed doors, windows, countertops, and display cases and took what they wanted. The items taken were not milk, eggs, and bread, bare necessities of life. They were expensive fashions, accessories, jewelry. etc., most of which were offered for sale by the grabbers soon afterward.

In some parts of our country, notably in Southern California, local district attorneys practiced no bail, though few criminals were even arrested. For weeks and months toward the end of the year, thieves could enter a store, take what they wanted, and were not susceptible to arrest if the value of stolen articles was less than $950. Drug stores like Walgreens made national news reports, more than a few closed for good because of such soft-on-crime policies and lenient judges who would not punish such things.

The Biden administration put blame largely on the COVID pandemic. As late as December 15, the press secretary answered the "Why?" question by a focus on the needs of people because of the coronavirus and variant mutations which were named by health officials. What blind eyes! What inaction on the part of the federal government!

Based on reports from 12,000 law enforcement organizations, the FBI's Preliminary Uniform Crime Report shows a 15 percent increase in numbers and non-negligent manslaughter in 2020" (AMAC). In 2021, murders in twenty-nine major cities jumped another 16 percent over the previous year's highs.

Southern California was not alone in such statistics. Homicides in Philadelphia, Pennsylvania stood at 503 with half a month of the year still to come. Indianapolis, Indiana had 240 homicides at that juncture, Columbus, Ohio (186), Louisville, Kentucky (187), and Austin, Texas (88), shamed four other large cities in the top ten.

AMAC (Association of Mature American Citizens) hastened to report that these were all Democrat-led cities. In Los Angeles, as of mid-year, homicides were up 36 percent. In Portland, Oregon, up 82 percent. And in Minneapolis, up 72 percent. Atlanta, Georgia, Chicago, Illinois, and Dallas, Texas were not much better. Houston, Orlando, and Pittsburgh rates were up. Reports were not good even in small cities like Rochester, New York.

Defunding the police was a hot topic for much of 2020 and 2021. Police, once watch dogs for our safety, were not only handcuffed by local restrictions, they were abused by activists in our cities, many of them injured. There were record retirements and policemen and women moved to other locations. Ambushes and killings of police were real (and continued to make morning news stories, at least, on some news networks).

In late December of 2021, Texas leadership decided to continue construction of the border wall, started by President Trump, but halted by Joe Biden. Border crossings at various spots climbed to preposterous highs. The "open border" policies of the Democrat politicians compounded the lack of law enforcement, not just in Texas and Arizona. Illegal entry to our country, with little or no vetting, no checking of COVID symptoms, and busing illegals to all parts of the nation, often under cover of night, exacerbated the problem.

Fentanyl, heroin, meth, cocaine, and synthetic narcotics crossed our borders unabated, few such detected and little apprehension of the offenders. There was "a 30 percent jump in drug overdose deaths, with 93,000 young people dead as a result." (Charles).

"Equity" was the buzzword for liberal politicians and progressive news sources. Not all imprisoned criminals actually got rehabilitated while serving their time. But for a decade or more, prisoners, some hardened criminals, were released from detention in the effort to be equitable.

Extra! Extra!

A book that includes a section on "the other thing" must have a story on extraterrestrials, right?

Extraterrestrials might be defined as alien life or life from outer space, especially if an intelligent being. Extraterrestrials are always characterized as fictional or hypothetical. There is no conclusive evidence of such life forms.

Of course, there are many believers. Many believe that extraterrestrials are already here, living among us. Such beliefs are thousands of years old, so I'll limit the questions to "recent" history, say 6,000 years ago up to the 2020s.

If you look for quotes on UFOs and alien life on Earth, the quotes are most likely from adamant believers in them.

Arthur C. Clarke, a co-writer for the screenplay for the movie *2001: A Space Odyssey* and English science fiction writer said, "There are two possibilities: either we are alone in the universe or we are not. Both are equally terrifying."[36]

Personally, neither is terrifying. If extraterrestrials exist, I'd like to know what their interest in our planet is all about. I'd have other questions, of course, but first, some other quotes.

Extra! Extra!

Ben Rich, sometimes called "the father of stealth," said, "There are two types of UFOs-the ones we build and the ones they build." Rich was an American engineer who worked on the development of many American aircraft.[37]

Stephen Hawking? I might have guessed otherwise, but he said, "I can discount reports of UFOs. Why would they only appear to cranks and weirdos?"[38]

Carl Sagan, astronomer, astrophysicist, writer, and planetary scientist has a quote a bit more ambiguous: "The reliable cases are uninteresting and the interesting ones are unreliable."[39]

So, are extraterrestrials "a thing" or not? One statistic says that believers are about three in ten. I put myself among the seven in ten. Why?

1. I'm from Missouri! You know, the "Show me" thing?

2. I'm a Bible believer. Nothing comes close to suggesting such life forms exist in the scriptures, written over four hundred centuries.

3. All of the supposed sightings fall into the fast-moving, mysterious lights, round or undetermined shapes, flying up there somewhere, never having made contact with the earthlings. True, some UFOs appear to hover, and then go away.

4. The life forms suggested are human-like, but with alien figures lacking color, pale or white with big heads and eyes. Check the Halloween costumes at any Walmart any year.

5. Back to the Bible, I don't read any reports of spaceships either leaving our planet or landing here. Surely, that would have been big news in Genesis and/or Revelations!

6. We've been to the moon. We're going to Mars in unmanned missions, and maybe manned, too. Civilian travel into space has started and will continue, and nothing untoward or extraterrestrial has been sighted. William Shatner would have leaked that info to someone, right?

Things That Happen In You

I read every day. I try to write every day, but writing requires more motivation. All of my reading and writing is done outside in fresh air and sunshine, no matter the air temperature. I often attribute escaping COVID for two years to my intake of sunshine vitamin D. Since early 2019, I've not been real careful avoiding crowds and public places. I keep those silly masks in my pocket or in the truck unless forced to wear them. Masks are for Halloween and Mardi Gras!

I'm surprised that many of my friends seem to be non-readers. Some of them may not be retired and work or have other things to do. I ride a bike five or six days a week, I'm always doing some gardening, and like everyone, I shop as needed and sometimes window shop just for something to do. Cooking for one is a challenge, but for the most part, that's enjoyable, too.

I've published eight books, have two more written, both awaiting available financing since my church pension and social security checks run a little short of expenses. I've convinced myself that selling books is far less important than writing them.

My reading is chiefly paperbacks from Sam's Club. Brad Meltzer, Lee Child, Stuart Woods, Harlan Coben, Nicholas Sparks, and a good bit of Grisham, Patterson, Box, Baldacci with occasional escapes to Sandra Brown, Lisa Jackson, Janet Evanovich, and other lady authors. Dalia Owens and J.D. Vance are great reading!

This, That and the Other Thing

The title of this book is a quirky thing. It came to me one sleepless night after lots of beer and pizza. It surprised me to see how many stories I could write (find) for "This, That, and the Other Thing" sections. Initially, "thing" was the operative word, but there's a lot of "this" and "that" stuff also if you think about it.

One hundred pages into *Fast Ice* (Clive Cussler and Graham Boun, G.P. Putnam's Sons, New York), I noticed a quote from Eric Butterworth (*Spiritual Economics*): "Things may happen around you, and things may happen to you, but the only things that really count are the things that happen in you."

Do you see how easy this is? A heretofore unnoticed quote results in the longest story in this book!

What's happening around us right now? To pick just a few, Vladimir Putin's horrific destruction of life and property in Ukraine, COVID still happening, maybe never to leave us? Illegal immigration is a thing now, and it doesn't need (have) to be! Inflation as spring has begun and summer approaches affect everyone with no end in sight.

I began driving at the age of fifteen, three score and four years ago. I remember getting gasoline for our '55 Chevy for nineteen cents a gallon. This afternoon, I got just over eleven gallons with a Sam's Club discount for four dollars a gallon. Unless the president has a change of mind (heart), we could be paying six or seven dollars a gallon by July!

One week ago, we had two hours of tense attention to tornado warnings in the early evening, one or more such storms touching down briefly just two miles from my house. Those were the storms that wiped-out many homes and businesses in Arabi, Louisiana in a neighboring parish.

I have a plumbing problem in the laundry room unless I take special precautions when I wash clothes. Some things you can live with for a while, but plumbing, whether laundry room, bathroom, or kitchen, require immediate fixing if and when you can afford them.

I'll be eighty in a few months. I can read nearly everything without glasses, but I did notice my vision can blur, especially while driving at night. So, I paid a bunch of money for lens replacement in both eyes in the last forty days. My healthcare provider regarded that surgery as cosmetic, so no help financially. You do what you gotta do!

Now the things that really count. I'll put these in the general realm of personal emotions. How do you react to the things that happen around you and to you? What happens "in" you?

Sometimes our reaction is positive, maybe love? Other times, quite the opposite, maybe hate? In the interest of brevity, I'm choosing just the good that happens in some of us: charity, cheerfulness, appreciation, joy, success, love, comfort, gratitude, relief, peace, thankfulness, happiness, etc.

Some are similar emotions: joy, cheerfulness, happiness. To be brief, I'll choose just three of these: appreciation, comfort, and thanksgiving.

Appreciation has limitless possibilities. I'm a birder, gardener, garage sale nut, and baseball fanatic. I have a family of house wrens that must have a nest in my carport, iron fencing near the front door. The wrens feed on a hanging suet block near the potted crape myrtle tree. Since they hop around near the ground and around other potted treasures, there must be seeds and other foods there that keep them happy. The suet feeder is also frequented by red-headed woodpeckers, chickadees, gold finches, jays, and even mockingbirds. The several baby wrens have as many shades of brown as the Sherwin Williams store. House wrens have an erect tail that sticks up at a 45 degree angle and twitches when they see me watching them. The wrens have as big a voice as any bird in my yard, with the possible exception of crows that fly over each day.

An arm extended three feet from where I sit can brush a potted blackberry bush, now full of white blooms and near-to bust buds that will yield many thumb-size purple-black berries in less than a month. The canes extend five feet in several directions, honey bees busily working nine to five every day. There's a large berry patch also in the backyard.

When Martin Luther explained the fourth Petition of the Lord's Prayer in his *Small Catechism*, he said, "All that belongs to the support and wants of the body." His list included good neighbors. My street has a park to the north, an open field to the south, and thirty homes. Since Hurricane Katrina (2005), the street and the neighborhood have become mixed, some couples, and a number of families with children. Though first and last names may not be known or used, we acknowledge one another, sometimes stop to talk, and we watch out for each other. I especially appreciate Barbara, next door, who regularly offers meals. She cooks for one, too. I talk mostly with Judy across the street, and Judy who lives next to Michael, all four of us without a spouse. I am truly fortunate with these aspects of daily bread.

Not everyone can speak well of their health. I have stopped counting how many kidney stone episodes I've endured, but except for those, my health is regularly appreciated. For a long time now, I have taken nothing but a baby aspirin daily, with no ill effects. I've had excellent doctors and almost always feel quite good. Dentistry also has been a real blessing; nothing happening in my mouth for years, twice a year visits, of course. My disposition about going to the dentist is wholly different now than it was as a teen!

Comfort? Maybe you have to be retired to be comfortable for or with certain mundane things. After a fairly fast one-hour bike ride, do you know the comfort I find and feel is a cushioned lawn chair, though sweaty, for the half-hour cooldown? I find comfort in the two and a half hour drive to visit my daughter in Lafayette, and stay for the night before comfortably driving home again. I feel real comfort planting vegetables and nurturing them, and in the harvest. Bird watching, trimming the grass at the curb and the sidewalks, finding firewood on the street for later use.

Reading a good book, and watching a few favorite TV shows. Doesn't everyone feel comfort and security when tired and the head hits the pillow? Occasional beach stays, a gentle rain shower, beautiful sunrises and sunsets, enjoyable music, the Sunday church respite, and talking with friends? You experience these comforts, too, right?

Thanksgiving? This story could get real lengthy! Other parts of this book delineate my "thank you, Lord" recalls. I bet you can't list just one, but you do need the time to stop and smell the roses!

Something About A Sunday

Do the days of the week have a certain feeling? Does a Monday feel any different than a Thursday? What does a Wednesday feel like versus, say, a Friday? On which day of the week do you feel best of all? Are the feelings pretty much the same with everyone or do daily feelings depend on the individual?

If you are not going to school, not gainfully employed, homeless, or maybe even retired, the days of the week may not make a lot of difference to you. If you worship regularly, whether on Saturdays, Sundays, or other worship days, those days are likely quite different, maybe even to the point of a day of rest. So, there are considerations and/or suppositions involved in answering the questions above.

What is your favorite day of the week? The least favorite because of the feelings you have on those?

For many working people (hospitality workers, restaurant owners and workers, dairy farmers and ranchers, lawn care workers, people in the military, students in school, etc.), Mondays might be the least favorite day. You come from two days off the grind to back to the grind. For those, Wednesdays might be regarded as hump day (halfway to the weekend), and Fridays maybe TGIF!

Something About A Sunday

There's a really interesting story about Kris Kristofferson and Johnny Cash, and the country song "Sunday Morning Coming Down." Kristofferson wrote the song, first recorded by Ray Stevens, but popularized by Johnny Cash (2004), #1 on the Billboard Hot Country Singles Chart. Part of the lyrics attempts to capture the feeling of a Sunday morning after too much drinking and smoking and substances even more stunning the mind and body on Saturday night. Johnny Cash sang, "There's something about a Sunday that makes a body feel alone."

Kris Kristofferson was an Oxford graduate, a Rhodes Scholar, an army captain, and a helicopter pilot. With a resume like that, Kristofferson's real interest and desire was to be a song writer. It is said that his parents disowned him for what they thought was a futile love and senseless devotion to the music industry, never their family ties.

With successes in education, in the military, and the sky's the limit, Kristofferson found himself sweeping floors in Nashville at Columbia Records. There were attempts to get the attention of Johnny Cash, the just-by-chance walk-bys (meetings) never happening, but Kristofferson persisted with his dreams and real love.

Kristofferson tried a new angle. He befriended Johnny's wife, June Carter. She saw the talent and got some of the writing into the hands of the "man in black," but to no avail.

Now, things got a little foggy, like many misty Tennessee early mornings and like numerous Kristofferson foggy mornings. His plan was to fly a helicopter to the Cash home, which he apparently did while on an Army Reserve trip.

Sometimes you have to take such a chance. This chance apparently was successful as Kristofferson and Cash became friends. Cash invited Kristofferson to perform with him on stage at the Newport Folk Festival. They performed together for years as part of The Highway Men.

Kristofferson had many well-known songs, performed and recorded by many country music stars, among them "Me and Molly McGee," "For the Good Times," "Help Me Make It Through the Night," and "Sunday Morning Coming Down."

At this writing, Kristofferson is eighty-six years old. He has said he'd like the first line of Leonard Cohen's "Bird on the Wire" on his tombstone:

"Like the bird on the wire,
Like a drunk in a midnight choir,
I have tried in my way to be free."

Coming down on a Sunday morning, feeling so lonesome, I think I know what that "something" might be, what might be missing, what might help.

Every Little Thing Is Gonna Be Alright

The jingle on the Sandals Resorts commercial, which shows beautiful beaches and Caribbean waters, is sung with the message, "Every little thing is gonna be alright."

What a pitch for the American public who, in late August of 2022, have put up with two or more years of COVID lockdown, inflation near 10 percent, gas prices doubled of what they were not long ago, invasion of immigrants unabated, crime that seems to go totally unpunished, exorbitant spending by a Democrat administration, a CDC that has lost the trust of the American people. I could go on with other displeasure and disappointment. What about all "the big things" affecting us every day? Gonna be okay?

Can a vacation, even for just one week, make everything okay? Probably not, but it sure would be nice to get away. "Honey, write that phone number down and let's get out of town!"

What are the vacation spots that Americans, at least, the citizens of the country, want to visit? The mountains? An amusement park? A family visit out of state? A beautiful beach? Barbados? Antigua? Montego Bay? Mexico? Europe?

One thing about the Sandals resorts that must be considered, aside from the costs, is that these are resorts for couples. Everything is included in the daily rates: limitless gourmet dining, all of the drinks and entertainment you'd want, spas, pools, steam rooms, water sports, fresh water lakes, golf, certified scuba diving onsite, snorkeling, all tips, taxes, and gratuities, and more! The one thing not included? The kids!

The Sandals Resorts for couples began in 1981, and now have sixteen locations in the Caribbean. Ten thousand employees take care of your "every little thing." The Sandals Grenada is perhaps the best of the bunch. The Regency La Toc gives you a choice of twenty-seven restaurants. Wow! Dinner for two weeks; one better than the next!

My wife died twelve years ago. Since I don't have a current lady friend, I think if Sandals allows singles, I'd feel very much out of place. I did not request cost for any of the locations. Somehow, I think that would be a determining factor for me, too. I'm quite comfortable with every little thing on occasional stays in Missouri, Texas, and Florida. The nation's problems will likely not be okay when the respite, no matter where, ends!

If It's Not One Thing, It's Another

"Folks are usually about as happy as they make up their minds to be," Abraham Lincoln. You're just past Baton Rouge, another hour and you'll be at your daughter's house in Lafayette.

You note the odometer as you check mileage on the truck, 44,800, remembering that on Monday, you'll get that brake job that has been postponed for five weeks. The oil change was last done at 40,000 miles, so new oil and filter is needed now. And did the guy at Firestone say the two front tires needed replacing? The oil change can be done for $50, but tires? If you can catch a deal, $100 each. And the brake job? Maybe $700?

In late winter 2023, Ash Wednesday next week already; inflation is eating up the budgeted food prices (pun intended), gas prices are still double of one year ago, your one dress suit hardly fits any more, and you really should schedule that Life Line health screening with the clinic. It's not easy to keep your eyes on the road, your hands on the wheel. If it's not one thing, it's another! But life goes on.

Where does that saying come from? Everyone feels the distraction and deals with the scenarios of life. "Misery loves company" is not a comfort as you cross the Mississippi River and hope that your daughter's distractions are less than yours.

You are retired. You've been keeping up with house maintenance, the front and back yards, the main appliances still hum in the quiet times of early morning and late at night. Your fixed income hasn't changed in ten years, though. There have been slight increases in social security not resulting in increased quality of life. But life goes on.

Neighbors and friends sometimes share their situations and dilemmas. The single mom with two kids about to go to high school, one having braces and the other needing braces. The oldest has a required special diet because of allergies. Her social life could use an upgrade, but personal wants are sacrificed because, like others, she wants the best for her children. But life goes on.

The young couple in church "live" on one salary, his job in the oil and gas industry lost two years ago in Texas. He works hard, but income from the new job is far less than satisfies needs. Three young children, all with private school costs, clothing, and each active in school sports. Travel costs on one weekend sometimes match the work week travel costs for both parents. Expenses get cut, yet paycheck to paycheck somehow still works each month and year. But life goes on.

Quality of life? That doesn't necessarily depend on wealth. Some very wealthy folks are very unhappy in life. Leo Tolstoy: "If you want to be happy, be."

"If it's not one thing, it's another." The idiom is used when bad things keep happening to you. I think the operative word to focus on here is "bad." There's another idiom that applies: "We are all (well, most of us) in the same boat." You are not the only one who has had to deal with inflated costs, the need for new tires and servicing the family car(s). The loss of a job, health problems, family conflict, braces for the kids, etc. Is that comforting? Of course not! But it is true. How you (we) deal with those life issues determines our happiness, success, contentment, and accomplishments.

What if you (we) think of the opposite to the bad? What about the "good" things that happen to us? Focus on the things that we can and should be thankful for?

Not everyone has (or can have) children. Maybe everyone or most folks in our neighborhood have a car, but many have no family or personal vehicle(s). YOU (We) see folks lying under an overpass, clutching a sleeping bag or an old blanket in the cruelest of weather conditions. Not everyone has a shelter from the storm. Not everyone has a good (or even okay) retirement. Not everyone is in good (or even okay) health. Not everyone has one or more friends. Many have no family. Another story (title) in this book ("This Day, Give Us Bread") is apropos to our quality of life.

I'll end this story on a sobering, sorrowful, and (I'll venture) an even negative note as at the start of this story: Life goes on. Or does it?

Albert Einstein, a genius, right? His simple thought: A table, a chair, a bowl of fruit, and a violin. What else does a man need to be happy?'

Ever try to catch a butterfly without a large net? Nathaniel Hawthorne: "Happiness is like a butterfly, which, when pursued, is always beyond our grasp, but if you will sit down quietly, may alight upon you."

Anything You Can Do I Can Do Better

Most folks have no difficulty finishing that saying. "Anything you can do I can do better." The saying and the song prompt many thoughts and a variety of scenarios. Most of us experience some superiority if truthful to self.

It's early in the 2022 NFL football season. Though the individual football players may not be so bold, their fans debate who is best unashamedly. ls it Tom Brady? ls it Aaron Rogers? Everyone has his/her favorite. All of the teams dream about postseason playoff games. Some even dream of Super Bowl prospects before the season begins. There are thirty-two NFL teams.

In baseball, there are BIG stories and comparisons, as well. Aaron Judge of the Yankees has hit sixty-two home runs in the regular season. Albert Pujols of the St. Louis Cardinals finished his last season in the sport, having joined the 700 Home Run Club, joining only Bobby Bonds, Hank Aaron, and Babe Ruth to claim that honor.

Some say the Los Angeles Dodgers will win the World Series. Others say the Houston Astros.

The Atlanta Braves will have something to say about those claims. And other MLB teams arc inclined to say: "Anything you can do we can do better."

Imagine the claims for best or better among the pizza chains. The fast food burger businesses? Coca-Cola and Pepsi? The national political parties vie for best or better in the November elections and again in 2024.

Ford, Chevrolet, and many other automobile manufacturing contenders? The Emmys and the Oscars? The World Cup soccer teams? There is no lack of competition for the top spot in so many venues. We guess that is good, free enterprise!

Any of the above could result in an argument, right? As the song lyrics say, after the "Anything you can do, I can do better" line, "No, you can't!" "Yes, I can!" "No, you can't!" "Yes, I can!"

Ethel Merman sang the song long ago (1946), the show tune composed by Irving Berlin for the Broadway musical *Annie Get Your Gun*. Many other versions of the song followed. The braggadocio is often repeated in families at home, ball teams on the field or the court, students of any age in schools, office workers, sales people, barbeque experts, NASCAR crews, the American Kennel Club owners and enthusiasts, major horse breeders, trainers, and jockeys, ad infinitum.

Endnotes

1. Historical.ha.com/itm/books/children

2. worldstopexports.com/pork

3. quest-thoughtco.com/def

4. https://en.wikipedia.org/wiki/The_Impossible_Dream_(The_Quest)#:~:text=%22The%20Impossible%20Dream%20(The%20Quest,name%20starring%20Peter%20O'Toole.

5. Merriam-Webster.com Dictionary, s.v. "crisis," accessed August 18, 2023, https://www.merriam-webster.com/dictionary/crisis.

6. https://www.goodreads.com/quotes/search?utf8=%E2%9C%93&q=You+never+want+a+serious+crisis+to+go+to+waste.&commit=Search

7. Youssef, Michael. Hope for This Present Crisis: The Seven-Step Path to Restoring a World Gone Mad. United States: Charisma Media, 2021.

8. https://archive.org/details/78_this-is-my-country_vaughn-monroe-and-his-orchestra-fred-wise-albert-frisch_gbia0132215a

9. https://hbr.org/2011/08/henry-ford-never-said-the-fast

10. https://www.goodreads.com/quotes/49502-i-alone-cannot-change-the-world-but-i-can-cast

11. The Commission on Worship of the LC-MS, 2006, Concordia Publishing House, St. Louis, Missouri

12. https://www.worldhistory.org/article/1900/luthers-speech-at-the-diet-of-worms/

13. https://www.shmoop.com/quotes/this-is-the-city.html

14. https://en.wikipedia.org/wiki/List_of_cities_by_homicide_rate

15. https://www.smithsonianmag.com/air-space-magazine/how-much-worlds-population-has-flown-airplane-180957719/

16. https://afdc.energy.gov/data/10331#:~:text=The%20United%20States%20is%20the,while%20Brazil%20primarily%20uses%20sugarcane.

17. http://www.songlyrics.com/cline-dion/so-this-is-christmas-lyrics/

18. Merriam-Webster.com Dictionary, s.v. "aha moment," accessed August 18, 2023, https://www.merriam-webster.com/dictionary/aha%20moment.

19. Merriam-Webster.com Dictionary, s.v. "moment," accessed August 18, 2023, https://www.merriam-webster.com/dictionary/moment.

20. https://en.wikipedia.org/wiki/Life_Is_Just_a_Bowl_of_Cherries

21. https://en.wikipedia.org/wiki/That%27s_Life_(song)

22. https://genius.com/Kenny-loggins-this-is-it-lyrics

23. https://www.gordonconwell.edu/center-for-global-christianity/

24. Merriam-Webster.com Dictionary, s.v. "conjugation," accessed August 19, 2023, https://www.merriam-webster.com/dictionary/conjugation.

25. The Lutheran Hymnal, (Concordia Publishing House, St. Louis, Missouri, 1941).

26. https://www.imdb.com/title/tt0083131/quotes/

27. https://en.wikipedia.org/wiki/Song_Sung_Blue

28. https://genius.com/Willie-nelson-hello-walls-lyrics

29. https://www.google.com/books/edition/The_Book_of_Useless_Information/YsEZP61FqDsC?hl=en&gbpv=0

Endnotes

30 https://www.google.com/books/edition/That_s_Entertainment/9VpWAAAAMAAJ?hl=en&gbpv=0&bsq=That%27s%20Entertainment

31 https://genius.com/Buddy-holly-thatll-be-the-day-lyrics

32 https://genius.com/Louis-armstrong-when-the-saints-go-marching-in-lyrics

33 https://vpc.org/?gclid=Cj0KCQjw0IGnBhDUARIsAMwFDLna9F-vuIf-HTppjUIDv-_LhN8SFV0Wb1YUGdh2HqrflrL_d0MmKfgkaAh-woEALw_wcB

34 https://www.wdsu.com/article/new-orleans-ends-2021-with-218-murders-well-never-get-over-this/38646625

35 https://en.wikipedia.org/wiki/Robert_B._Charles

36 https://en.wikipedia.org/wiki/Arthur_C._Clarke

37 www.gaia.com/article/ben-rich-lockheed-martin-and-UFOs

38 libquotes.com/stephen-hawking/quote

39 https://quotefancy.com/quote/783107/Carl-Sagan-UFOs-The-reliable-cases-are-uninteresting-and-in-the-interesting-cases-are

Printed in the USA
CPSIA information can be obtained
at www.ICGtesting.com
LVHW040824011023
759730LV00030B/125